Inspiring Asian Americans

30 Role Models That Shaped Our World
-- Past & Present

Mari Yamaguchi

Edited by Monica Baker

Cover design by Kostis Pavlou

1st Edition 2024

For my future grandchildren

CONTENTS

WELCOME TO OUR FAMILY

Welcome to *Inspiring Asian Americans: 30 Role Models That Shaped Our World!*

The story of Asian Americans in the United States is a long and interesting one. It's full of challenges, successes, and important contributions to our country.

The first major wave of Asian immigrants came to America in the mid-1800s. Many came looking for new opportunities, like the Chinese miners who joined the California Gold Rush in 1849. Others, like Manjiro, arrived by chance and found a new home. In 1843, he was a 14-year-old fisherman and the first Japanese person to arrive in the U.S.

These early immigrants faced many difficulties. There were unfair laws that made it hard for Asian people to enter the country or become citizens. Those who did make it here often faced discrimination and harsh treatment.

But Asian immigrants didn't give up. They helped build the railroad across America, started businesses, and fought for their rights. For example, in 1885, the Tape family won an important court case that said Chinese American children had the right to go to public schools in California.

Over time, more Asian immigrants came to America from different countries. In 1965, a new law made it easier for Asian immigrants to come to America, which is why we see so many diverse Asian American communities nowadays. Today, over 20 million Asian Americans—about 7% of the U.S. population—have roots in more than 20 countries across Asia and India.

As an Asian American, I want other Asian Americans to know that this history belongs to all of us, no matter which Asian country our families came from. Whether a family has been in America for a long time or a person is a new immigrant, we're all part of the Asian American community. We share many common experiences and our stories are an important part of our country's story.

But what does it mean to be Asian American? Or just American, of whatever descent? These are big questions that many of us think about. It's like trying to figure out where you fit in a big puzzle of different cultures and backgrounds. Here's what I've learned:

Being American isn't about where you were born. It's about choosing America as your home, contributing to its society, and being part of its ongoing story. Many of the people in this book weren't born in the U.S., but they *chose* to live here and have made our country better. That makes them just as American as anyone born here.

Your accent (or not having an accent) doesn't define your American-ness, either. Even those of us Asian Americans born and raised in the U.S. sometimes face questions like, "Where are you really from?" Or misguided compliments like, "You have no accent!"—even if English was the only language we ever spoke. This can make us feel like we don't belong in our own country. But remember ... we are just as American as anyone else, no matter how we speak or look.

Asian Americans sometimes get put into categories that aren't fair. On one hand, they're sometimes seen as the "model minority"—hardworking, education-focused, and high-achieving. While this might seem positive, it can also make their struggles invisible and divide them from other minority groups. On the other hand, some people treat Asian Americans like we're not *really* American. But we're so much more than these simple categories and stereotypes.

The 30 Asian Americans in this book show how diverse and amazing the Asian American community is. They've done great things in science, art, sports, politics, and more. They've broken barriers, stood up for what's right, and made the world better in big and small ways.

I've tried to include people from many different Asian backgrounds in this book. But please don't worry about how many people are from one particular ethnic group compared to others. Some Asian groups have a longer history in the United States, so they might have more people included here. That's only because it takes time for communities to establish themselves in a new country.

What's most important is that all these people are part of a shared American story. As you read their stories, look for things they have in common. What qualities helped them succeed? How did they overcome challenges? What impact did they have on their communities and the world?

Most importantly, how might their stories inspire *you*?

FILM AND ENTERTAINMENT

PEOPLE IN FRONT OF AND BEHIND THE CAMERA

ANNA MAY WONG

HOLLYWOOD'S FIRST CHINESE AMERICAN STAR (1905-1961)

A s Hollywood's first Chinese American movie star, Anna May Wong opened doors for Asian actors in the U.S. film industry. Her talent and determination to leapfrog racism and discrimination made her an inspiration for generations of Asian Americans in the entertainment world and beyond.

A Childhood Dream

Anna May Wong was born Wong Liu Tsong in Los Angeles, California on January 3, 1905. Her parents were second-generation Chinese Americans who ran a laundry business. Growing up, Anna May lived in a diverse neighborhood with Chinese, Irish, German, and Japanese families.

From a young age, Anna May would often skip school and use her lunch money to go to the cinema. She was passionate about films! At just nine years old, she decided she wanted to become an actress. She even came up with her stage name, "Anna May Wong," by combining her English and Chinese names!

Breaking into Hollywood

How would you guess a young Chinese American girl in the early 1900s would ever get to star in movies? For Anna May, it started with being an extra. At 14, she appeared in her first film, *The Red Lantern*. From there she took any role she could get, even if it meant just standing in the background.

Anna May's hard work paid off, and in 1922, she landed the lead role in *The Toll of the Sea*. This was one of the first movies in color, and 17-year-old Anna May's performance earned her praise from critics. This was her big break.

Challenges and Stereotypes

Anna May was incredibly talented, but she still faced challenges in Hollywood. In the 1920s and 1930s, there was a lot of discrimination against Asian Americans. Many roles for Chinese characters were given to white actors who would wear makeup to look Asian! This practice was called "yellowface."

When she did get roles, they were often stereotypical and didn't show the full range of who Chinese people really were. Anna May was usually cast as either a "dragon lady"—a villainous, scheming character, or a "butterfly"—a submissive, self-sacrificing woman. One of her biggest disappointments came when she wasn't cast as the lead in *The Good Earth*, a movie about Chinese farmers. Instead, the role went to a white actress in yellowface.

Making Her Mark in Europe

The roles for Asian Americans in Hollywood were so limited that a frustrated Anna May decided to try her luck in Europe. She made movies in Germany, France, and England and became a big star! In London, she even performed in a play with the young Laurence Olivier, who later became one of the most famous actors in the world.

In Europe, Anna May was seen as a fashion icon. Then in 1934, she was named "The World's Best-Dressed Woman" by the Mayfair Mannequin Society of New York. She was recognized not just for her acting, but also for her style.

Standing Up for Better Representation

Throughout her career, Anna May spoke out against the stereotypical roles given to Chinese actors. In a 1933 interview, she said, "Why is it that the screen Chinese is always the villain? And so crude a villain—murderous, treacherous, a snake in the grass! We are not like that. How could we be, with a civilization that is so many times older than the West?"

Anna May used her fame to challenge these stereotypes. She turned down roles that she felt were demeaning to Chinese people. By choosing her roles carefully she hoped to change how Asian Americans were represented in movies and in real life.

Breaking New Ground

Despite the challenges, Anna May achieved many firsts in her career:

- She was the first Asian American to lead a U.S. television show. In 1951, she starred in *The Gallery of Madame Liu-Tsong*, playing a Chinese art dealer who solves mysteries.

- She was one of the first Asian American actresses to gain international recognition.

- In 1960, she became the first Asian American to receive a star on the Hollywood Walk of Fame.

Anna May's achievements opened doors for future generations of Asian American actors and actresses.

Beyond Acting

Anna May was an actress, but she was also a voice for her community.

During World War II, she raised money to help China in its fight against Japan. She even wrote a preface for one of the first Chinese cookbooks in America, raising money for United China Relief. By 1936 Anna May wanted to learn more about her heritage and took a year-long trip to China. She wrote articles about her experiences for American newspapers, helping to bridge understanding between Chinese and American cultures.

Lasting Legacy

Anna May Wong passed away in 1961, but her impact continues to be felt today. She proved that Asian Americans could be stars in Hollywood, even when it wasn't easy. Her determination to challenge stereotypes and push for better representation paved the way for the diverse actors we see on screen today.

What Ideas Influenced Anna May?

In 2022, Anna May Wong became the first Asian American to appear on U.S. currency when her image was featured on a quarter as part of the American Women Quarters Program.

This honor recognizes her important place in American history and culture, propelled by the relatively simple ideas that influenced her:

1. Asian Americans could and should be stars in Hollywood.

2. Stereotypes should be challenged.

3. Never give up.

Think About It

Anna May Wong once said, "I was so tired of the parts I had to play." Instead of giving up acting, she persevered and had the courage to fight for better roles and representation.

Next time you watch a movie or TV show with Asian American actors, remember the trailblazer Anna May Wong.

What would *you* do if you faced unfair treatment because of who or what you are? How do you think you can use your talents to make a positive change in the world?

BRUCE LEE

THE LITTLE DRAGON WHO CHANGED THE WORLD (1940-1973)

B ecoming a legend requires extraordinary talent, unwavering determination, and the power to inspire millions. The legend Bruce Lee had all of that. His journey from a scrappy Hong Kong street fighter to an international icon is a story that will make you believe anything is possible.

Early Life: A Star is Born

Bruce Lee was born on November 27, 1940, in San Francisco, California. His parents were visiting from Hong Kong, where his father was a famous opera singer. His birth name was Lee Jun-fan, which means "return again" in Chinese. His parents gave him this name hoping he would return to the United States when he grew up.

When Bruce was just a few months old, his family returned to Hong Kong. Growing up there wasn't easy. During World War II, Hong Kong was occupied by Japan, and life was tough for everyone. But even as a young boy, Bruce showed a fighting spirit that would define his whole life.

A Troubled Teen Finds His Path

As a teenager, Bruce got into a lot of fights. He was small for his age, but he had a fiery temper and wasn't afraid to stand up to bullies. His parents worried about him and wanted him to channel his energy in a positive way. That's when Bruce started learning Wing Chun kung fu from the famous master Ip Man.

Bruce threw himself into martial arts training. He practiced for hours every day, determined to become the best he could be. But life had other plans for him. When he was 18, Bruce got into a serious fight, and his parents decided it would be safer for him to move back to America.

Coming to America: New Challenges

Bruce left behind everything he knew. He moved to Seattle, Washington, and worked as a waiter in a Chinese restaurant while finishing high school. Afterwards, he enrolled at the University of Washington to study philosophy.

But Bruce never stopped practicing martial arts. In fact, he started teaching other students his own style, which he called Jun Fan Gung Fu. He believed that martial arts weren't just about fighting—they were a way to express yourself and grow as a person.

Breaking Barriers in Hollywood

Bruce dreamed of becoming an actor, but in the 1960s, most Asian characters were still played by white actors in yellowface. The few Asian actors who did get parts were often stuck playing stereotypes.

But Bruce refused to accept this. He believed he could change things. He got his first big break playing Kato in the TV series *The Green Hornet*. Even though Kato was supposed to be the sidekick, Bruce's expert martial arts skills and charisma made him the real star of the show.

Creating a New Martial Art: Jeet Kune Do

Bruce wasn't satisfied with traditional martial arts. He believed that many of them were too rigid and didn't work well in real fights. So, he created his own martial art—not just style—called Jeet Kune Do, which means "The Way of the Intercepting Fist."

Jeet Kune Do was revolutionary. Instead of following strict rules and forms, it encouraged students to adapt and use whatever worked best for them.

"Be water, my friend. Empty your mind. Be formless, shapeless, like water. You put water into a cup, it becomes the cup. You put water into a bottle, it becomes the bottle. You put it in a teapot, it becomes the teapot. Now, water can flow or it can crash. Be water, my friend."

Bruce's idea of being flexible and adaptable like water wasn't just about martial arts—it was a philosophy for life. He encouraged people to find their own path and not be limited by traditions or expectations.

Becoming a Global Superstar

In the early 1970s, Bruce returned to Hong Kong to make movies. His films *The Big Boss*, *Fist of Fury*, and *Way of the Dragon* were huge hits across Asia. But it was his last completed movie, filmed in Los Angeles and Hong Kong, that made him a global superstar.

Enter the Dragon was the first martial arts film produced by a major Hollywood studio. It showcased Bruce's skills and charisma to the world. But sadly, he died suddenly just days before the movie was released in 1973, at the young age of 32.

A Lasting Legacy

Bruce Lee's short life has had an enormous impact on the world. He helped change the way Asian Americans were seen in movies and TV, paving the way for future generations of actors. His philosophy of self-expression and personal growth through martial arts has inspired millions of people around the world.

But Bruce's influence goes far beyond martial arts and movies. He showed that an Asian American could become a global icon, breaking down stereotypes and cultural barriers. His dedication to constant self-improvement and his refusal to accept limitations continue to inspire people of all backgrounds.

Fun Fact: Bruce Lee's famous and tight "one-inch punch" was so powerful it could send a person flying backward. He developed this technique to show that power doesn't always come from big movements.

What Ideas Influenced Bruce Lee?

Bruce once said, "I hope to free my comrades from bondage to old ideas and set a pattern for an approach to all styles and schools." He was talking beyond martial arts—he was encouraging everyone to think for themselves and find their own path in life.

His life was short, but his impact continues to be felt around the world. Here are a few things Bruce believed:

1. Don't let others define you.

2. Be adaptable, like water taking the shape of its container.

3. Express yourself.

Think About It

Bruce Lee said, "The key to immortality is first living a life worth remembering."

What dreams do you have for your life? What barriers do you see in your own life? How can you be like water, adapting and flowing around obstacles?

KEN JEONG

FROM DOCTOR TO COMEDY STAR (1969-)

K en Jeong, comedian and actor in the TV show *Community*, makes us laugh so hard our sides hurt. But behind Ken is a surprising story: before his Hollywood fame, he was a medical doctor. From medicine to entertainment, Ken has a tale of following passion, overcoming obstacles, and using his unique talents to reinvent himself.

Early Life and Education

Kendrick Kang-Joh Jeong was born on July 13, 1969, in Detroit, Michigan, to parents who had immigrated from South Korea in search of new opportunities. When Ken was four years old, his family moved to Greensboro, North Carolina.

Growing up, Ken was incredibly smart and hardworking. At Walter Hines Page High School, he excelled in Quiz Bowl and the student council, and, if that wasn't enough, he played violin in the school orchestra.

Ken's academic abilities were so impressive that he graduated from high school in 1986 at the age of 16—two years earlier than most students! After receiving the Greensboro Youth of the Year award, he moved on to Duke University for college and the University of North Carolina for medical school. In 1995, he realized his dream and earned his M.D. (Doctor of Medicine) degree.

The Comedy Bug Bites

Now, you might be thinking, "Wait a minute! I thought Ken Jeong was a famous comedian and actor!" Well, here's where Ken's story gets really interesting!

Even while he was studying to be a doctor, Ken had a secret passion—comedy. During his summer break before medical school, he took theater classes at the University of California, Los Angeles (UCLA), and caught a bug he couldn't ignore.

While completing his medical residency in New Orleans, Ken started performing at open mic nights at local comedy clubs. In 1995, he even won a comedy competition called the Big Easy Laff-Off. The contest judges were so impressed by Ken's talent that they encouraged him to move to Los Angeles to pursue comedy professionally.

A Difficult Decision

After finishing his medical training, Ken faced a big decision. Should he stick with the safe and respected career as a doctor that he had worked so hard for, or should he take a risk and try to make it in the competitive world of entertainment?

In 1998, Ken decided to do both! He moved to Los Angeles to work as a hospital doctor during the day. But at night and on weekends, he performed stand-up comedy at famous clubs like The Improv and Laugh Factory. Can you imagine how busy and tired he must have been, balancing these two *very* different jobs?

The Big Break

Ken's hard work and talent in comedy began to pay off. He started getting small roles on popular TV shows like *The Office, Entourage*, and *Curb Your Enthusiasm*. But his big break came in 2007 when he was cast in the movie *Knocked Up* as ... a cranky doctor!

The success of *Knocked Up* gave Ken the confidence to make a life-changing decision. In 2006, he left his medical practice to pursue acting and comedy full-time. It was a risky move, but Ken believed in himself and his abilities.

Rising Star

Ken's gamble paid off in a big way. In 2009, he landed two roles that would make him famous around the world. First, he was cast as the hilarious and unpredictable Spanish teacher Señor Chang on the TV show *Community*. Then, he played the outrageous Mr. Chow in the blockbuster movie *The Hangover*.*

These performances showcased Ken's unique comedic talents and made him a household name. He went on to appear in many more movies and TV shows, including *Crazy Rich Asians, The Masked Singer*, and his own sitcom, *Dr. Ken*.

The Hangover movies are rated R and contain adult material that may not be suitable for minors.

More Than Just Funny

While Ken is best known for making people laugh, there's much more to him than his comedy. He uses his fame to raise awareness for important causes and to represent Asian Americans in the entertainment industry. And did you know that Ken keeps his medical license active?

Even though he doesn't practice medicine anymore, he believes it's important to maintain skills he worked hard to master. During a stand-up comedy show in 2018, an audience member suffered a medical emergency. Ken jumped off the stage to help the person until paramedics arrived. Now *that's* what we call a multi-talented performer!

Ken has also been open about his wife's battle with breast cancer, using his platform to encourage people to get regular check-ups and support cancer research. His ability to find humor even in difficult situations has inspired many people facing similar challenges.

What Ideas Influence Ken Jeong?

Ken Jeong's journey from doctor to comedy star is a powerful reminder that it's never too late to follow your dreams. Here's what he once said about his career change:

"I always go back to this mantra that my wife had when she was going through chemotherapy: 'If you're not living on the edge, you're taking up too much space.' I was living on the edge when I quit my job to do stand-up. I was living on the edge when I did *The Hangover*. I did not know that it would lead to all this."

We can see these ideas influence Ken's actions:

1. Taking risks can lead to amazing opportunities.

2. A person can have multiple passions. Follow them all!

3. Keep up skills that you've mastered.

Think About It

Like Ken Jeong's, our backgrounds and experiences can shape our future in unexpected ways. Ken's medical knowledge often comes in handy when he's acting or doing comedy, and his sense of humor surely made him a better doctor, too.

The skills and knowledge you gain now might be useful in ways you can't even yet imagine.

What are your passions? How might you combine different interests to create a unique path for yourself?

MINDY KALING

FROM COMEDY WRITER TO HOLLYWOOD POWERHOUSE (1979-)

Many people dream of creating a hit TV show or writing a bestselling book. Mindy Kaling has done both. This Asian American superstar is a comedian, actress, writer, and producer who's breaking barriers and making people laugh along the way.

Early Life and Passion for Comedy

Vera Mindy Chokalingam, known professionally as Mindy Kaling, was born on June 24, 1979, in Cambridge, Massachusetts. Her parents were both immigrants from India—Mindy's father worked as an architect, while her mother was a doctor.

Mindy was always a smart and creative kid who loved to make people laugh. She attended the Buckingham Browne & Nichols school, where she discovered her passion for writing and spent her free time creating her own comic strips or performing in school plays. Popular TV shows like *Saturday Night Live* and *Frasier* inspired her to one day become part of the entertainment world herself.

Fun Fact: Mindy's parents named her after the TV character Mindy from the show *Mork & Mindy*. They wanted to give her a "cute American name!"

College Years and Early Career

After graduating high school in 1997, Mindy headed to Dartmouth College. There, she jumped into her creative side. She joined an improvisational comedy group called The Dog Day Players and even produced her own comic strip for the college newspaper.

But Mindy's college experience wasn't all fun and games. While many of her classmates were planning steady careers in business or medicine, Mindy knew she wanted to pursue her passion for comedy and writing. It takes a lot of courage to follow an unpredictable and unconventional path, doesn't it?

After graduating from Dartmouth in 2001, Mindy moved to New York City to be close to the entertainment industry. She worked various jobs, including as a production assistant on a TV show, while also performing stand-up comedy at night. It wasn't always easy, but Mindy's determination kept her going after her dreams.

The Big Break: *The Office*

Mindy's hard work paid off when she got her big break in 2004. She was hired as a writer and performer for a new TV show called *The Office*.

At just 24 years old, Mindy was the only woman on a writing staff of eight people. She created the character of Kelly Kapoor, a bubbly and talkative customer service representative, who soon became a fan favorite on the show. Mindy shined as an actor in *The Office* but also wrote many episodes, showing off her talents both in front of and behind the camera.

Creating Her Own Show: *The Mindy Project*

After years of success on *The Office*, Mindy was ready for a new challenge. In 2012, she created, wrote, produced, and starred in her own TV show called *The Mindy Project*. In it, a young doctor tries to balance her personal and professional life, inspired by Mindy's own experiences growing up as the daughter of immigrant parents.

Creating your own TV show is a huge accomplishment for anyone, but it was especially significant for Mindy. As an Indian American woman, she was breaking new ground in the entertainment industry. *The Mindy Project* ran for six seasons and helped pave the way for more diverse voices in television.

Expanding Her Reach: Books, Movies, and More Shows

Mindy's talents go beyond just television. She's also a bestselling author! She's written two New York Times best-selling memoirs, *Is Everyone Hanging Out Without Me? (And Other Concerns)* and *Why Not Me?* In these books, Mindy shares funny stories from her life meant to inspire readers to follow their dreams.

But wait, there's more! Mindy has also appeared in several movies, including *A Wrinkle in Time* and *Ocean's 8*. She's even voice-acted in animated films like *Inside Out* and *Wreck-It Ralph*.

Mindy continues to create new TV shows. She co-created the Netflix series *Never Have I Ever*, which tells the story of an Indian American teenager navigating high school. She also created *The Sex Lives of College Girls* for HBO Max. Through these shows, Mindy helps showcase diverse stories and represent people who haven't always seen people who look like themselves on TV.

Inspiring Others and Breaking Barriers

Mindy has certainly faced challenges, including dealing with sexism and racism in the entertainment industry. She chooses to use her experiences to fuel her creativity, push for change, and open doors for others. She often hires diverse writers and actors for her shows, giving opportunities to people who might not otherwise get them in Hollywood.

"Work hard, know your stuff, show your stuff, and then feel entitled," she once said.

Mindy's attitude has helped her overcome obstacles, stay in the game, and become a huge success.

What Ideas Influence Mindy Kaling?

Today, Mindy Kaling is recognized as one of the most influential people in entertainment. She's won numerous awards, including Screen Actors Guild Awards, and has been nominated for Emmy Awards six times. In 2022, she even received the National Medal of Arts from President Joe Biden, one of the highest honors for artists in the United States.

But, perhaps the most positive impact Mindy has had on young people, especially Asian Americans, is more important than her awards. She's shown that it's possible to succeed in Hollywood while staying true to yourself and your heritage.

Mindy lives by some very sound ideas:

1. Follow your dreams ... with hard work!

2. Know your stuff—build your expertise.

3. Stay true to yourself and to your heritage.

Think About It

Mindy Kaling started out just like you—a kid with big dreams and a love for making people laugh.

As you read about her journey, what parts of Mindy's story inspire you the most? Do you have dreams that might seem challenging to achieve?

What are your passions? How do you think you can use your talents to make a positive impact on the world, just like Mindy has done with her writing and acting?

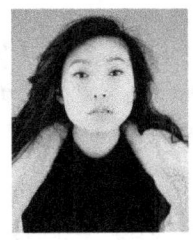

AWKWAFINA

FROM YOUTUBE RAPPER TO HOLLYWOOD STAR (1988-)

One of the most exciting talents in entertainment today is an actress and rapper born as Nora Lum. Better known as Awkwafina, she rose to fame with her quick wit, unique voice, and fearless attitude.

A Childhood Filled with Music and Laughter

Nora Lum was born on June 2, 1988, in Stony Brook, New York. Her father is Chinese American, and her mother was Korean American. Sadly, Nora's mother passed away when she was only four years old. After that, she was raised by her father and grandmother in Forest Hills, Queens.

Growing up, Nora found comfort and joy in music. She learned to play the trumpet and studied classical music and jazz at the famous Fiorello

H. LaGuardia High School of Music & Art and Performing Arts. (If you've seen the movie "Fame," that's the school it was based on!)

But Nora loved hip-hop, too! At age 13, she started rapping and creating her own beats using computer programs. One day, this hobby would lead to an exciting career.

Creating Awkwafina: A New Identity

When Nora was 15, she came up with a new name for herself: Awkwafina. She said that Awkwafina was like an alter ego—a more confident and outgoing version of herself. It was like having an avatar that helped her overcome her shyness and eventually led her to stardom.

After high school, Awkwafina attended the University at Albany, where she studied journalism and women's studies. But she kept her love for music and comedy. In fact, it was during college that she wrote a song that would change her life.

YouTube Fame and Early Career

Later, in 2012 when she was 24, Awkwafina uploaded a rap song called "My Vag" to YouTube. The song was funny and uniquely daring, and the video quickly went viral. She became an internet sensation!

Ahh, but fame comes with challenges! Awkwafina was fired from her job at a publishing house when her boss recognized her from the video. She didn't let this setback stop her, though.

She kept making music and released her first album, *Yellow Ranger*, in 2014. She also started appearing on shows like *Girl Code* on MTV. Slowly but surely, she was making her way into the entertainment world.

Breaking into Hollywood

Awkwafina's big break in movies came in 2018 when she appeared in two major films: *Ocean's 8* and *Crazy Rich Asians*. In *Crazy Rich Asians*, she played Goh Peik Lin, a funny and outgoing character who quickly became a fan favorite. Her performance made audiences and critics take notice—this new star had something special!

But it was her role in the 2019 movie *The Farewell* that really proved Awkwafina as a standout actress. In the film, she played Billi, a young woman visiting her sick grandmother in China. This more serious role was a big change from her usual comedy parts, but Awkwafina won a Golden Globe Award for Best Actress for her performance. She was the first person of Asian descent to win a Golden Globe for lead actress in a movie!

When she accepted the award, Awkwafina pointed to it and said, "If I fall upon hard times, I can sell this, so that's good."

A Multi-Talented Star

One of the coolest things about Awkwafina is that she doesn't just do one thing—she's a true multi-talent!

She acts in movies, makes music, writes, and even creates her own TV shows. She's also an animated movie talent. Awkwafina has voice-acted in movies like *Raya and the Last Dragon* and *The Little Mermaid* where she shows off her quick wit and humor by improvising many of her lines. In the Marvel superhero universe, she plays Katy in *Shang-Chi and the Legend of the Ten Rings*.

In 2020, Awkwafina created, wrote, and starred in her own TV series called *Awkwafina is Nora from Queens*. By making this show, Awkwafina is telling her own story and also giving opportunities to other Asian American actors and writers to work on the show.

Breaking Barriers and Inspiring Others

Here's what Awkwafina once said about representation in movies and TV:

"I think that the more we have stories that show diverse faces and diverse stories, it's going to change the way that we see our world. And that's what's so important."

Awkwafina has helped increase representation of Asian Americans in entertainment through her variety of roles. She shows that Asian Americans can be funny, dramatic, and everything in between. Her journey reminds us that it's important to see people who look like us doing amazing things. It helps us believe that we can do those things, too!

Challenges and Growth

Of course, Awkwafina's path hasn't always been smooth. She's faced criticism for some of her early work and has had to learn and grow in the public eye. But instead of getting defensive, Awkwafina has shown a willingness to listen and learn from others.

What Ideas Influence Awkwafina?

Awkwafina's ideas for success are good for all of us:

1. Don't be afraid to be yourself, even if that means being a little "awkward" sometimes.

2. Hard work and persistence can lead to amazing opportunities.

3. It's possible to have multiple talents and interests—you don't have to choose just one!

4. Representation matters—seeing people who look like you succeed can inspire you to chase your own dreams.

Think About It

Awkwafina started out as a regular kid from Queens who loved music and making people laugh. Now, she's a Hollywood star who's changing the way we see Asian Americans on screen.

As you read about Awkwafina's journey, what parts of her story inspire you the most? Do you have talents or interests that you'd like to pursue, even if they seem unusual or challenging?

What dreams do you have? How do you think you can use your talents to make a positive impact on the world, just like Awkwafina has done with her acting and music?

JAMES WONG HOWE

THE WIZARD OF LIGHT AND SHADOW
(1899-1976)

H ave you ever been mesmerized by what you saw on a movie screen? The lighting, the shadows dancing, the overall magic? If so, you might have James Wong Howe to thank! He was a master cinematographer—the person responsible for how a movie looks on screen—who changed the way we see movies forever.

A Journey from China to America

James Wong Howe was born in 1899 in Guangdong, China. When he was just five years old, his father sent for James and his mother to join him in America. The Howe family settled in Pasco, Washington, where they owned a general store.

Like many Asian immigrants in early 1900s America, James faced discrimination and struggled to fit in. But he was curious and determined to succeed. When his father bought him a Brownie camera, young James became fascinated with photography. That simple gift would change the course of his life and cinematic history!

From Delivery Boy to Hollywood Legend

James's journey to becoming one of Hollywood's most respected cinematographers wasn't a straight line.

As a teenager, he tried professional boxing, then moved to Los Angeles to become a pilot. When that didn't work out, James took on odd jobs, including as a delivery boy for a photography studio. There, James had a chance encounter that would change his life. He met someone working on a movie set and managed to get a job as a camera assistant. This was his foot in the door to the film industry!

James learned everything he could about cameras and lighting. One day, while taking publicity photos of a famous actress named Mary Miles Minter, James made an accidental discovery. He noticed that her blue eyes photographed darker and more striking when she was looking at a dark surface. This simple observation led to his first big innovation in cinematography.

Soon, he was in high demand.

Mastering the Art of Light and Shadow

James Wong Howe quickly gained a reputation as a master of light and shadow. His innovative techniques helped define the look of *film noir*, a style of movie known for its dark, mysterious atmosphere.

But he didn't stop there. James experimented and pushed the boundaries of what was possible with a camera. Here are some of his amazing innovations:

1. The "Howe Black": He used black velvet around the camera to make actors' eyes look more dramatic on film.

2. Low-key lighting: James created lighting based on dramatic shadows—sometimes by using only candlelight, which was technically challenging—earning him the nickname "Low-Key Howe."

3. Moving cameras: He created one of the first camera dollies—a wheeled platform that allows smooth camera movement. For boxing scenes in movies, he would put on roller skates and film with a handheld camera as he glided around the ring.

4. Deep-focus cinematography: This technique keeps both close and far-away objects in focus at the same time, creating a more realistic image.

5. Wide-angle lenses: These lenses allowed for more of the scene to be captured, giving a fuller view of the world on screen.

Breaking Barriers in Hollywood

Despite his incredible talent, James Wong Howe faced many challenges because of his race. When he first came to America, Chinese people weren't allowed to become citizens. It wasn't until 1943, when James was in his 40s, that he was finally able to become an American citizen.

James also fell in love with a white woman named Sanora Babb. But at that time, it was against the law in California for people of different races to marry. They traveled all the way to Paris to get married in 1937, and their marriage wasn't legally recognized in California until 1948!

During the 1950s, James was "grey-listed" because some people thought he might have communist sympathies.* This made it hard for him to find work for a while, but he never gave up on his passion for filmmaking.

Despite these obstacles, James persevered and worked on over 130 films—from westerns to science fiction—during his career. He won two Academy Awards and was nominated for eight more, making him one of the most celebrated cinematographers in film history.

*During the 1950s, many Chinese Americans faced unfair treatment because of the "Red Scare"—an intense fear of Communism. People wrongly thought that anyone with Chinese ancestry might be connected to Communists, even if they weren't. This led to harsher discrimination against Chinese Americans simply because of their family background.

Legacy of Light

James Wong Howe passed away in 1976 and is remembered as one of the greatest and most influential cinematographers of all time. He is also remembered for helping to open doors for other Asian Americans in Hollywood. James taught and mentored young cinematographers, including other minorities who also faced discrimination in the industry.

His innovative spirit and dedication to his craft continue to inspire people in the film industry. In fact, the Association of Asian-Pacific American Artists created an award in his honor called "The Jimmie" to recognize excellence in filmmaking.

What Ideas Influenced James Wong Howe?

James Wong Howe once said, "You have to have a point of view. That's the only way to make a picture that's different." Here are some ideas that might influence his point of view:

1. Curiosity can lead to amazing things.

2. Don't be afraid to experiment.

3. Hard work and talent can overcome prejudice.

4. It's important to share your knowledge.

Think About It

Having your own unique perspective and the courage to express it can help you stand out and make a difference in whatever you choose to do. So, the next time you watch a movie, pay attention to how it looks—the lighting, the shadows, the way the camera moves. Think about how these elements help tell the story.

And ... remember James Wong Howe, the Chinese American who helped shape the way we see movies.

ANG LEE

TELLING STORIES THROUGH FILM (1954-)

G reat filmmaking has the power to transport viewers to entirely new worlds, and Ang Lee is a true master of the art.

Dreaming of Hollywood in Taiwan

Ang Lee grew up in a place where becoming a movie director wasn't considered a "real" job. Born in 1954 Taiwan, young Ang was expected to focus on traditional subjects in school. His father wanted him to become a professor, but schoolwork was not his strong suit. He failed the college entrance exam twice, which was a huge disappointment to his family.

But Ang had a secret passion—he loved movies and how they moved people emotionally with stories. So, he made a bold move...

A Dream Takes Flight

In 1979, when he was 23 years old, Ang left Taiwan for the United States to study film at the University of Illinois and later at New York University. Lee had to learn a new language and adapt to a new culture. But his determination and love for filmmaking kept him going.

After graduating, Lee couldn't find work in the film industry. For six years, he stayed at home taking care of his two children while his wife worked to support the family, but Ang didn't give up on his dream. He used the time to write screenplays and develop his film ideas.

Breaking Through

Lee's big break came in 1991 at the age of 37, when he directed his first feature film, *Pushing Hands*. His films started to gain attention around the world, and in 1993 and 1994, he won the top prize at the Berlin International Film Festival—two years in a row was a rare achievement! His films *The Wedding Banquet* and *Eat Drink Man Woman* explored the clash between traditional Chinese values and modern Western ideas, drawing from Lee's own immigrant experiences.

These early films were successful in Taiwan and caught the attention of Hollywood. Soon, Lee was directing big-budget English-language films. One of his most famous early Hollywood movies was *Sense and Sensibility*, based on the classic novel by Jane Austen. People doubted whether an Asian director could successfully make a British period drama. But the film was a huge success and won many awards, showing that Lee could adapt to different cultures and storytelling styles.

A Filmmaker Without Borders

Ang Lee has accomplished something that no other Asian director has done—he's won the Academy Award for Best Director *twice*!

What makes him special as a filmmaker? He doesn't stick to just one type of movie or story. Let's look at some of his most famous films:

- *Crouching Tiger, Hidden Dragon* (2000): This kung-fu movie combines impressive action scenes with a touching story about love and honor. Winning an Oscar for Best Foreign Language Film, it's one of the most successful non-English language films ever made in the United States and the highest-grossing in many countries.

- *Brokeback Mountain* (2005): This groundbreaking film tells a sensitive love story between two cowboys. It won Lee his first Academy Award (Oscar) for Best Director.

- *Life of Pi* (2012): Based on a popular book, this visually stunning movie follows the adventure of a boy stranded on a lifeboat with a tiger. It won Lee his second Oscar for Best Director.

From action-packed adventures to deeply emotional dramas, Lee is a curious explorer, always ready to try something new.

Pushing Boundaries

Technically, Ang Lee looks for ways to make movies more exciting and immersive for audiences. He's experimented with 3D technology and even tried making a movie that plays at a much higher frame rate than usual, making the images look super realistic.

But it's not just about fancy technology for Lee. He cares deeply about the stories he tells and the characters in his films. He once said, "I'm not a native speaker of the language of Hollywood, but I try to read it and understand it and make it work for me."

Lee sees filmmaking as a way to bridge different cultures and experiences.

Overcoming Challenges

On his journey to success, Lee faced language barriers, cultural differ-ences, and discrimination as an Asian filmmaker in Hollywood. Some people doubted whether he could understand and portray stories from cultures different from his own. But he saw this as an advantage.

"I'm a mixture of many things," he once said. "I'm an outsider, but I've been around. I think I can see things from different angles."

Lee uses his unique perspective to bring fresh ideas to his films. He shows that great stories can cross cultural boundaries and touch peo-ple's hearts, no matter where they're from. And he takes risks. Lee is not afraid to try new things, even if they might fail. Even so, after his movie *Hulk* failed in 2003, Lee considered retiring. But his father encouraged him to keep making movies. Lee listened and went on to create some of his most successful and acclaimed films after that setback.

What Ideas Influence Ang Lee?

Lee once said, "You have to use your cultural background to tell stories, but you also have to find the part of you that's universal."

This idea is at the heart of Lee's work. He believes that while our cultural backgrounds shape us, we all share common human experiences and emotions. That, along with the following ideas, has shaped his life:

1. Don't be afraid to dream big.

2. Persistence pays off.

3. Embrace your unique perspective.

4. Challenge yourself.

Think About It

Ang Lee's journey from a young movie lover in Taiwan to an Oscar-winning director in Hollywood is truly inspiring. He shows us that with creativity, hard work, and the courage to tell your own stories, you can achieve amazing things.

"I try to please everyone, but I also try to challenge everyone."

What do you think you can do to please and challenge the world with your unique talents?

MUSIC, ART, AND DESIGN

CREATORS OF SOUND, SIGHT, AND STYLE

MINORU YAMASAKI

THE ARCHITECT WHO BUILT DREAMS TO THE SKY (1912-1986)

Minoru Yamasaki was one of the brilliant minds who created the modern, towering skyscrapers. He designed over 250 buildings during his career, including the original World Trade Center in New York City.

From Humble Beginnings to Architectural Star

Born in Seattle, Washington, on December 1, 1912, Minoru was the son of Japanese immigrants. Growing up, he and his family worked hard but didn't have much money, and there was much discrimination against Japanese Americans at the time.

But Minoru had a dream. He loved to draw and was fascinated by buildings. Minoru graduated from the University of Washington with a degree in architecture in 1934. Even so, finding work as an Asian American architect during the Great Depression* was tough. With just $40 in his pocket, he made the bold decision to move to New York City to chase that dream.

*The Great Depression was a really tough time in the 1930s when many people lost their jobs, didn't have enough money, and struggled to buy food and other basics. It affected countries all around the world and lasted for about 10 years.

Overcoming Obstacles

In New York, Minoru took odd jobs, like wrapping dishes for an import company. He continued to study and improve his architecture skills, even while working full-time. Eventually, he found work as a draftsman, drawing building plans for other architects.

During World War II, Minoru faced a new difficulty. Many Japanese Americans were being sent to internment camps* because of fear and prejudice. Luckily, Minoru's employers helped him avoid internment, and he was even able to bring his parents to New York to keep them safe. He also worked to help relocate Japanese Americans affected by the internment program. Even while facing discrimination himself, Minoru wanted to make a difference for others.

His experiences influenced his architectural philosophy. He once said, "I feel this is the outstanding characteristic of our democracy—that we have a society that is fluid, able to change, and able to keep its doors open for the development of talent, wherever that talent may appear."

*During World War II, the United States and Japan were enemies. Sadly, this led the U.S. government to make a terrible decision. They forced over 110,000 people of Japanese origin, the majority of them U.S. citizens, to leave their homes and live in guarded camps called internment camps. Most *of these people had done nothing wrong and were loyal to America. The government's action was based on fear and prejudice, not facts. Years later, the U.S. admitted this was a big mistake and formally apologized.*

Rising to the Top of His Field

After the war, Minoru moved to Detroit and started his own architecture firm. He ended up designing buildings all over the world, from airports, to universities, to skyscrapers. People loved his unique style. His designs often mixed modern styles with elements inspired by nature and traditional architecture from around the world.

Some of Minoru's most famous early works include the Pacific Science Center in Seattle, with its lacy arches, and the Dhahran International Airport in Saudi Arabia, which appears on Saudi money!

But his biggest project was yet to come.

The World Trade Center: A Towering Achievement

In 1962, Minoru was chosen to design the World Trade Center in New York City. This was a huge honor. The Twin Towers would be the tallest buildings in the world at that time!

Designing the World Trade Center was a big challenge. Minoru and his team had to solve many problems:

1. How to make the elevators work efficiently in such tall buildings?

2. How to keep the buildings from swaying too much in the wind?

3. How to create a strong foundation in the soft soil of lower Manhattan?

They came up with innovative solutions to these problems, and the World Trade Center* was completed in 1973, becoming one of the most recognizable landmarks in the world. Minoru Yamasaki proved he could tackle even the biggest architectural challenges.

Tragically, on September 11, 2001, the towers were destroyed in a terrorist attack. This event, often called "9/11," deeply affected America and the world. Today, a new World Trade Center stands in their place, symbolizing hope and remembrance.

Challenges and Criticism

Not everything in Minoru's career was perfect. Some of his projects faced serious problems and were eventually torn down. The World Trade Center, while famous, was also criticized by some for its design when it was built.

But Minoru kept learning and adapting throughout his career. He wasn't afraid to try new ideas or to admit when something failed. But there was one glitch: he was afraid of heights! That's right—the man who designed some of the tallest buildings in the world didn't like being up high himself. That's why many of his skyscrapers have narrow windows. He designed them so people wouldn't feel scared looking out from high floors.

Legacy and Continued Influence

Minoru Yamasaki believed that buildings should create feelings of "serenity, surprise, and delight" in the people who used them. He wanted his architecture to make people's lives better and more beautiful. And it did.

Many of Minoru's buildings are still appreciated, admired, and studied by architects and students. In recent years, some of his buildings have been carefully restored, and in 2015, his McGregor Memorial Conference Center was named a National Historic Landmark.

Minoru's success opened doors for other Asian Americans in architecture and design. He showed that with talent, hard work, and determination, anyone could achieve great things, regardless of their background.

What Ideas Influenced Minoru Yamasaki?

If Minoru Yamasaki were alive today, he might tell us to:

1. Dream big.

2. Use your unique perspective to include your heritage.

3. Help others.

4. Face your fears, even if they include a fear of heights!

Think About It

Minoru's story shows that you can succeed in any field you choose, even if you don't see many people who look like you doing it. His creativity, problem-solving skills, and willingness to take on big challenges are qualities that can inspire all of us, no matter what career we want to pursue.

What kind of mark do you want to leave on the world? Whatever your dream is, remember Minoru Yamasaki's story, and don't be afraid to reach for the sky!

I.M. PEI

SHAPING THE WORLD THROUGH ARCHITECTURE (1917-2019)

Extraordinary buildings can inspire awe and wonder, especially the breathtaking structures of I.M. Pei. This famous Chinese American architect created some of the most iconic buildings of the 20th and 21st centuries, including the glass pyramid at the Louvre Museum in Paris and the Rock and Roll Hall of Fame in Cleveland.

Early Life and Background

Ieoh Ming Pei was born on April 26, 1917, in Guangzhou, China. As a young boy, Pei was surrounded by lush gardens and traditional buildings of Suzhou, where his family had roots. He loved the combination of the outdoors and ancient Chinese architecture that sparked his interest in design. But when Pei was 10, his family moved to Shanghai, a bustling big city filled with modern building designs from around the world.

He grew up with two completely different styles of architecture—the serene Chinese gardens and the towering skyscrapers of Shanghai. This unique blend of old and new would later inspire Pei's innovative designs.

In 1935, at the age of 17, Pei bravely left his home country to pursue his education in the United States. In America, he had to learn English, adapt to a new culture, and study hard to become an architect. But I.M. Pei didn't give up. He studied at the Massachusetts Institute of Technology (MIT) and later at Harvard University, where he learned from some of the greatest architects of the time.

Rising to the Top

After finishing his studies, Pei started working in New York City for a real estate developer. But Pei had bigger dreams—he wanted to design buildings that would inspire people and stand the test of time. In 1955, he started his own architectural firm, I.M. Pei & Associates. He quickly gained a reputation for his unique style, which combined modern designs with elements from traditional architecture. He often used materials like glass, steel, and concrete to create structures that seemed to defy gravity.

One of Pei's first major projects was the National Center for Atmospheric Research in Colorado, completed in 1967. Instead of creating a typical boxy building, Pei designed a structure that looked like it was part of the mountains around it. People loved it!

This project put Pei on the map as a talented and genius architect who could create stunning buildings that fit perfectly into their environment. But it was just the beginning of Pei's stupendous career.

Pei's determination and unique approach to architecture won him more and more prestigious projects. In 1983, he was awarded the Pritzker Prize, often called the "Nobel Prize of architecture." This award recognized Pei's incredible talent and cemented his place as one of the world's top architects.

The Louvre Pyramid: A Controversial Masterpiece

Have you ever seen pictures of a giant glass pyramid in front of an old French palace? That's one of Pei's most famous (*and* controversial) works—the entrance of the Louvre Museum in Paris, France. When the design was first revealed in 1984, many Parisians were outraged. They thought the modern pyramid would clash badly with the historic museum building.

But Pei stood by his design. He believed that the transparent pyramid would bring light and openness to the museum while respecting its history. Years later, he said, "If there's one thing I know I didn't do wrong, it's the Louvre."

Despite the initial backlash, Pei's Pyramid opened in 1989 and quickly became beloved by locals and tourists alike. The Louvre Pyramid has become a symbol of Paris—so much so that it's hard to imagine the Louvre without its iconic glass entrance anymore.

Reaching for the Sky: The Bank of China Tower

Another of Pei's creations is the Bank of China Tower in Hong Kong. This skyscraper looks like a bunch of glass triangles delicately stacked on top of each other, reaching high into the sky. Pei designed it to represent the growth of bamboo, a symbol of hope and prosperity in Chinese culture.

Building this tower wasn't easy. Hong Kong has strong winds and typhoons, so Pei had to make sure the building was super strong. He used a special design that made the building sturdy while still looking elegant and light.

A Lasting Legacy

I.M. Pei passed away in 2019 at the incredible age of 102, but his legacy lives on. He influenced architects and designed buildings all over the world, from museums in Germany and Qatar to skyscrapers in China and Singapore. Pei's buildings are known for their bold geometric shapes, use of natural light, and harmony with their surroundings.

Pei's work reminds us that architecture is more than just creating functional buildings—it's about shaping the way people interact with their environment and with each other. He once said, "The important thing is to create something that is not just for today but for tomorrow and the people of tomorrow."

Impact on the Asian American Community

I.M. Pei never forgot his roots. He used his success to open doors for other Asian American architects and designers, give back to his community, and bridge cultures between East and West.

After winning the Pritzker Prize, Pei used the prize money to create a scholarship for Chinese students to study architecture in the U.S.

What Ideas Influenced I.M. Pei?

What do you see in I.M. Pei's incredible life story? Here are a few possible takeaways:

1. Embrace your heritage.

2. Don't be afraid to think big.

3. Persevere in the face of criticism.

4. Use your success to help others.

5. Never stop learning and growing.

Think About It

Pei once said, "The important thing is to get the building right." This simple statement shows his dedication to creating the best possible designs, no matter the challenges.

The next time you see a stunning building, remember I.M. Pei and think about how you might leave your own mark on the world. What will you design? How will you shape the future? The possibilities are endless!

VERA WANG

DESIGNING DREAMS AND BREAKING BARRIERS
(1949-)

For decades, one of the world's most famous fashion designers has shared her remarkable gift of creating beauty that makes people feel special. This talented Asian American woman, Vera Wang, went from Olympic dreams to designing dresses worn by celebrities and brides around the world!

A Dreamer on Ice

Vera Ellen Wang was born on June 27, 1949, in New York City. Her parents had immigrated to the United States from China just a few years earlier. Vera's mother worked as a translator for the United Nations, while her father ran a successful medicine company. Growing up in New York, Vera had access to many exciting opportunities.

When Vera was eight years old, she discovered a passion that would shape her early life: figure skating. She began training seriously, spending her summers in Denver and the rest of the year practicing with the Skating Club of New York. Vera worked hard to improve her skills on the ice, dreaming of one day competing in the Olympics.

A Change of Direction

Despite her years of dedication, Vera faced a significant setback in her teens. In 1968, she competed in the U.S. Figure Skating Championships but didn't make the Olympic team. This was a huge disappointment for Vera.

Instead of stewing on her crushed Olympic dreams, Vera decided to pursue a different path. She attended Sarah Lawrence College, where she studied art history. During her time in college, Vera also spent a year studying at the University of Paris in France. This experience exposed her to the world of high fashion, which sparked a new interest.

Right after college, Vera landed a thrilling job as an editor at Vogue magazine. At just 21 years old, she was the youngest editor there! For 17 years, Vera worked hard at Vogue, learning everything she could about the fashion industry.

But Vera wasn't done growing and changing. In 1987, she left Vogue to work for the famous designer Ralph Lauren. This gave her hands-on experience in designing clothes and running a fashion business. After two years with Ralph Lauren, Vera was ready for her biggest challenge yet.

A Wedding Dress Revolution

When Vera was 40 years old, at the age when many people are settled in their careers, she decided to take a big risk. She left her job to start her own business designing wedding dresses. Why? Because when she was planning her own wedding, she couldn't find a dress she liked! Vera thought, "If I'm having this problem, other women must be, too." So, in 1990, she opened her first bridal boutique in New York City's Carlyle Hotel.

Vera's wedding dresses were different from what people were used to. They were modern and elegant and made brides feel like the best version of themselves. Soon, celebrities started wearing her dresses, and Vera Wang became a household name.

Becoming a Bridal Legend

Vera became known for creating gowns that were unique, elegant, and comfortable. Her designs were different from the puffy, princess-style dresses that were popular at the time. Instead, she made sleek, modern gowns that made brides feel sophisticated and special.

Some famous brides who have worn her designs include Kim Kardashian, Alicia Keys, Victoria Beckham, and even Ariana Grande! Vera's gowns have even appeared in popular TV shows and movies like *Sex and the City* and *Bride Wars*.

More Than Just Weddings

Vera didn't stop at wedding dresses. She expanded her brand to include a line of affordable wedding dresses called "White by Vera Wang." She makes ready-to-wear fashion for everyday life. Accessories like sunglasses and jewelry. Fragrances that smell amazing and home goods to make your house beautiful.

Even though Vera didn't become an Olympic skater herself, she found a way to combine her love of skating with her fashion career. She has designed costumes for several Olympic figure skaters, including Michelle Kwan and Nathan Chen. In 2009, Vera was inducted into the U.S. Figure

Skating Hall of Fame for her contributions to the sport as a costume designer.

Recognition and Success

Over the years, Vera Wang has received many awards for her work in fashion. Some of her biggest achievements include:

- Winning the Council of Fashion Designers of America (CFDA) Womenswear Designer of the Year in 2005

- Receiving the André Leon Talley Lifetime Achievement Award in 2006

- Being awarded the CFDA Lifetime Achievement Award in 2013

Vera's business has also been very successful. In 2018, her company's revenue reached $630 million, and Forbes magazine ranked her as one of America's richest self-made women.

In 2019, at the age of 70, Vera made a triumphant return to New York Fashion Week with a show celebrating her brand's 30th anniversary. The fashion world was amazed by her continued creativity and innovation.

Overcoming Challenges

Being a successful businesswoman isn't easy, especially in the competitive world of fashion. As an Asian American woman, Vera sometimes felt like an outsider in the fashion industry. Also, starting her own business at 40 was risky—many people thought she was too old to begin a new career. And finally, balancing work and family life was tough, especially as a mother of two adopted daughters.

But Vera never gave up. She worked hard, stayed true to her vision, and kept pushing forward. Today, Vera Wang is one of the most respected names in fashion.

What Ideas Influence Vera Wang?

Vera Wang lives by her own principles:

1. You can turn setbacks into new opportunities, no matter how old you are.

2. It's okay to change directions in life. Embrace the change!

3. Hard work and 100% effort pay off.

4. Creativity is invaluable.

Think About It

Vera Wang's journey from the ice rink to the runway is a testament to the power of pursuing your dreams, even if your path takes some unexpected turns along the way.

What dreams do you have? How could you turn your passion into a career someday? How could Vera Wang's story inspire you to pursue them?

YO-YO MA

THE CELLO MAESTRO WHO BRIDGES CULTURES (1955-)

M usic has the power to elevate the spirit, and when Yo-Yo Ma plays his cello, listeners often feel as if they're soaring. This world-famous musician isn't just a master of classical music—he's a cultural ambassador who uses his talent to bring people together from all corners of the globe.

A Child Prodigy

Yo-Yo Ma was born on October 7, 1955, in Paris, France. His parents were Chinese musicians who had moved to France during a difficult time in China's history. From the very beginning, music was a big part of Yo-Yo's life.

When Yo-Yo was just three years old, he started learning music. He tried playing the violin, piano, and viola, but none of them felt quite right. Then, at four years old, he discovered the cello. It was love at first sight ... or should we say, at first sound! From the very beginning, it was very clear that Yo-Yo was incredibly talented.

Moving to America and Growing Up

When Yo-Yo was seven, his family moved to New York City. This was a big change, but it opened up new opportunities for the young musician. There, he continued to amaze everyone with his musical abilities. He even played for two U.S. Presidents—Dwight D. Eisenhower and John F. Kennedy—before he was eight years old.

Like many kids who are really good at something, Yo-Yo sometimes felt different from his classmates. But he didn't let that stop him from pursuing his passion for music. As a teenager, Yo-Yo attended a special high school for talented young performers called the Professional Children's School. He graduated when he was only 15 years old! After that, he went on to study at the famous Juilliard School of Music.

But Yo-Yo wasn't just about music. He was curious about everything around him. This curiosity led him to study at Harvard University, where he graduated with a degree in anthropology. That study of human cultures would become very important in Yo-Yo's life and career.

A Musical Journey Around the World

As Yo-Yo grew up, he became one of the most famous cellists in the world. But what makes him truly special is the way he connects with people through his music.

"I'm always trying to figure out what makes music meaningful to people," he has said.

This curiosity has led him to explore all kinds of sounds and music, not just classical. He's played American bluegrass, traditional Chinese melodies, and Argentine tangos, and has even collaborated with rock musicians.

In 1998, Yo-Yo started a really cool project called the Silk Road Ensemble. Named after the ancient trade routes that connected Asia with Europe, this group brings together musicians from all over the world, playing all sorts of unusual instruments, to create new and exciting music. It's like a musical United Nations!

Yo-Yo speaks English, French, and Mandarin Chinese, but music is the language he uses to bring people from different backgrounds together. He's not just playing beautiful music; he's building bridges between people and cultures.

Music as a Force for Good

Yo-Yo Ma has recorded over 90 albums and won countless awards, including 19 Grammy Awards and the Presidential Medal of Freedom, which is the highest civilian honor in the United States. But for Yo-Yo, the real reward is using his music to make the world a better place.

After the tragic events of September 11, 2001, Yo-Yo played at the World Trade Center site to honor those who lost their lives. He's also performed at the inauguration of several U.S. Presidents, bringing his message of unity through music to millions of people. During the COVID-19 pandemic, when many people felt isolated and scared, Yo-Yo shared comforting music online. He even gave a mini-concert in a vaccine center after getting his COVID-19 shot, bringing joy to healthcare workers and patients!

Yo-Yo Ma believes that music can do more than just entertain people—it can actually make the world a better place. In 2006, he was named a United Nations Messenger of Peace. This means he uses his fame and talent to promote important causes like education and cultural understanding.

One of Yo-Yo's most inspiring projects is called "Bach Project." For this, he's playing all six of Bach's cello suites in 36 different places around the world. But it's not just about the concerts. In each place, he also spends a "Day of Action" working with local communities on projects that use culture to address social issues.

A Cello with a Story

Yo-Yo Ma's cello is almost as famous as he is. It's called the Davidov Stradivarius, and it was made way back in 1712 by a famous Italian instrument maker named Antonio Stradivari. This cello is over 300 years old and is worth millions of dollars!

But here's the cool part—Yo-Yo doesn't treat it like a museum piece. He plays it all over the world so people everywhere can enjoy its sound. He even calls it his "voice" because it helps him express his feelings through music.

What Ideas Influence Yo-Yo Ma?

Many ideas influence Yo-Yo Ma:

1. Follow your passion.

2. Keep learning, learn new styles, and collaborate with other people.

3. Use your talents to help others.

4. Embrace diversity.

5. Don't be afraid to try new things.

Think About It

Yo-Yo Ma's journey from a child prodigy to a world-renowned musician and cultural ambassador shows us that music has the power to cross boundaries, bring people together, and make a positive difference in the world.

What's your special talent? How could you use it to connect with others and make the world a little better, like Yo-Yo Ma does with his music?

MAYA LIN

SHAPING AMERICA'S MEMORIALS AND LANDSCAPES (1959-)

M aya Lin's journey will inspire you to dream big and never let others define your limits.

Who Is Maya Lin?

Maya Lin is an American architect, artist, and designer who has left an indelible mark on our nation's landscape. Her most famous work, the Vietnam Veterans Memorial in Washington D.C., was designed when she was just 21 years old! But that's only the beginning of her incredible journey.

A Childhood Filled with Creativity

Maya Ying Lin was born to Chinese immigrants on October 5, 1959, in Athens, Ohio. Her father, Henry Huan Lin, was a ceramicist and became the dean of the Ohio University College of Fine Arts. Her mother, Julia Chang Lin, was a poet and professor of literature at the same university.

Growing up in a household that valued art and education, Maya developed a love for both at an early age. She was a quiet child who enjoyed studying and spent a lot of time at home. While still in high school, Maya took courses at Ohio University where she learned to cast bronze in the school's foundry. This early exposure to art and design would shape her future in ways she couldn't yet imagine.

Fun Fact: Maya has said that she "didn't even realize" she was ethnically Chinese until later in life. It wasn't until her 30s that she became interested in exploring her cultural background.

Breaking Barriers: The Vietnam Veterans Memorial

After graduating high school, Maya went on to study architecture at Yale University. In 1981, when she was just 21 years old and still an undergraduate student, something extraordinary happened. Maya entered a national design competition for a new Vietnam Veterans Memorial to be built in Washington D.C. Her simple yet powerful design—a V-shaped wall of black granite inscribed with the names of fallen soldiers—won the competition out of 1,422 submissions!

Maya's design was unlike any war memorial that had come before it. She wanted to create a place for healing and reflection. In her own words, "I imagined taking a knife and cutting into the earth, opening it up, and with the passage of time, that initial violence and pain would heal."

Overcoming Challenges

Winning the competition was just the beginning of Maya's journey. When people found out that a young Asian American woman had designed the memorial, some were upset. They didn't think someone so young or someone of Asian descent should design such an important American monument.

Maya faced criticism and even racial insults. But she stood strong and defended her design before the U.S. Congress. She explained that the wall was meant to be like a cut in the earth, symbolizing the pain of the war. Eventually, a compromise was reached, and additional elements were added near her design. Her determination paid off, and the memorial was completed in 1982.

This experience taught Maya that "To fly, you have to have resistance." She learned that facing challenges head-on can make you stronger and help you achieve your goals.

The Power of Simplicity

Despite the initial controversy, the Vietnam Veterans Memorial has become one of the most visited sites in Washington, D.C. Millions of people come to see it each year, leaving personal items in memory of their loved ones. Maya's simple design turned out to be incredibly powerful, allowing people to reflect and heal.

This early success launched Maya's career, but it was just the beginning. She went on to design many other important memorials and public spaces, often exploring themes of history, social justice, and the environment. She has a unique ability to create spaces that make people think and feel deeply about important issues.

Nature as Inspiration

As Maya continued her work, she became more and more interested in the environment. Many of her later works focus on the relationship between people and nature. She draws inspiration from landscapes and tries to create a balance between human-made structures and the natural world.

Some of Maya's most famous works include: The Civil Rights Memorial in Montgomery, Alabama (1989), The Women's Table at Yale University (1993), The Wave Field at the University of Michigan (1995), and The Confluence Project along the Columbia River (2000-2008).

Maya once said, "I'm very much a product of the growing awareness about ecology and the environmental movement." She tries to create works that respect nature rather than trying to dominate it.

This connection to nature started in her childhood in rural Ohio. Growing up near ancient Native American earthworks sparked her imagination and influenced her later designs. Today, Maya uses her art and architecture to raise awareness about environmental issues like climate change and endangered species.

Continuing to Shape the Future

Even today, Maya Lin continues to create and inspire. She's working on what she calls her "final memorial"—a project called "What Is Missing?" This multi-platform artwork aims to raise awareness about the loss of biodiversity and natural habitats around the world.

What Ideas Influence Maya Lin?

Perhaps Maya reminded herself of these things as she pursued her dreams:

1. Don't be afraid to think differently—your unique ideas can change the world.

2. Face challenges with courage.

3. Connect with nature.

4. Use your talents, whatever they are, to make a difference.

Think About It

Maya encourages young people to think creatively and to care about the world around them. She believes that art and design can help us understand complex issues and imagine better futures.

She once said, "To me, the American Dream is being able to follow your own personal calling. To be able to do what you want to do is incredible freedom."

Have you thought about your natural talents? Are there any that you might want to pursue as you grow up?

SCIENCE &
TECHNOLOGY

PIONEERS AND INNOVATORS

CHIEN-SHIUNG WU

THE FIRST LADY OF PHYSICS (1912-1997)

K nown as the "First Lady of Physics," the brilliant Chien-Shiung Wu broke barriers and made groundbreaking discoveries that shaped modern physics. Her story is one of determination, intelligence, and the power of following your passion.

Early Life and Education

Chien-Shiung Wu was born on May 31, 1912, in a small town called Liuhe, in China. Even as a little girl, Wu showed a deep curiosity about how things worked and loved listening to the radio and learning about science. She was encouraged by her parents, who believed in education for both boys and girls— something that wasn't common in China at that time.

At just 11 years old, Chien-Shiung left home to attend a boarding school 50 miles away then went on to study physics at National Central University in Nanjing. She became a top student and even got involved in student politics, leading protests for democracy.

Journey to America and Early Career

After graduating, Chien-Shiung knew she wanted to continue her studies in the United States. In 1936, at 24 years old, she sailed across the ocean to America by ship. It was a big step for a young woman from China, but Chien-Shiung was determined to follow her passion for physics.

Chien-Shiung was brave and determined. She ended up at the University of California, Berkeley, where she impressed her professors with her brilliant mind. When World War II broke out, Chien-Shiung's adventure in America took an unexpected turn. In 1944, she joined a top-secret project called the Manhattan Project. Scientists on this project were working to develop the world's first atomic bomb.

Chien-Shiung's expertise in physics was crucial to the project. She helped solve a major problem with nuclear reactors by identifying a problem element called xenon-135.

Her work was so important that the famous physicist Enrico Fermi would say, "Ask Miss Wu" when they encountered difficult problems. Though Chien-Shiung later felt conflicted about the destructive power of nuclear weapons, her contributions to science were undeniable.

After the war, Chien-Shiung Wu became a professor at Columbia University in New York City. She was the first woman to become a tenured—for life—physics professor in the university's history! This was a huge achievement at a time when very few women worked in science, especially physics.

Groundbreaking Discoveries

Chien-Shiung's most famous experiment came in 1956. Two other scientists, Tsung-Dao Lee and Chen Ning Yang had a theory about something called "conservation of parity" in particle physics. But they needed someone to prove it experimentally. Who did they turn to? Chien-Shiung Wu!

Chien-Shiung designed and carried out an incredibly complex experiment. First, she cooled radioactive cobalt to extremely low temperatures and used powerful magnets. It was like trying to observe something incredibly tiny and fast-moving ... in slow motion!

The results of Chien-Shiung's experiment shocked the scientific world. She demonstrated that parity, a fundamental concept in physics long believed to be a universal law, does not always hold true in nature. This discovery completely changed our understanding of how the universe works at its most basic level.

Chien-Shiung's work was recognized by scientists around the world. She became known as the "First Lady of Physics" and the "Queen of Nuclear Research."

A Legacy of Inspiration

Despite her incredible achievements, Chien-Shiung faced many challenges. As a woman and an immigrant in a field dominated by men, she often experienced discrimination. When Lee and Yang—both men—won the Nobel Prize for the theory Chien-Shiung had proven, she was left out of the award. Many scientists felt this was unfair and that she deserved equal recognition.

But Chien-Shiung didn't let these setbacks stop her. She continued to make important discoveries throughout her career. She once said, "It is shameful that there are so few women in science.... There is a misconception in America that women scientists are all dowdy spinsters. This is the fault of men."

Chien-Shiung's contributions to science went far beyond her famous parity experiment. She wrote an important textbook on beta decay (a type of radioactive decay) that is still used by scientists today. She also conducted research that helped improve our understanding of sickle cell anemia, a serious blood disorder.

Even though Chien-Shiung didn't win the Nobel Prize, she received many other prestigious awards throughout her career, including the National Medal of Science in 1975 and the Wolf Prize in Physics in 1978. She became the first woman to be elected to the American Physical Society, receive a doctorate in physics from Princeton University, and be appointed a full professor at Columbia University.

Chien-Shiung used her position to speak out against discrimination and to advocate for equality in science. She encouraged more women and girls to pursue careers in science and math. She once said, "I wonder whether the tiny atoms and nuclei, or the mathematical symbols, or the DNA molecules have any preference for either masculine or feminine treatment."

Fun Fact: Wu's legacy continues to inspire scientists around the world. There's even an asteroid named after her!

Impact on Asian American Community and Society

Chien-Shiung Wu's success proved that immigrants could make significant contributions to American scientific research. Her work during World War II also highlighted the important role Asian Americans played in the country's scientific and military efforts.

She was also known for her advocacy. She spoke out for human rights and against political oppression. She used her fame to draw attention to important issues, showing that scientists could also be powerful voices for social change.

What Ideas Influenced Chien-Shiung Wu?

Chien-Shiung Wu had strong ideas about pursuing success:

1. Never stop being curious and asking questions.

2. Don't let others define your limits – you can achieve great things regardless of your background.

3. Stand up for what you believe in, both in science and in society.

4. Your work can have an impact far beyond what you might imagine.

Think About It

As you think about your own future, remember Chien-Shiung's words: "Don't be afraid of hard work. Nothing worthwhile comes easily."

What do you think is worth working hard for?

STEVEN CHU

FROM LASER COOLING TO SAVING THE PLANET
(1948-)

The brilliant scientist and Nobel Prize winner Steven Chu has made groundbreaking discoveries and used his knowledge to address some of the world's most pressing issues.

A Curious Mind from the Start

Steven Chu was born on February 28, 1948, in St. Louis, Missouri. Steven grew up in a family that really valued learning—his father was a chemical engineering professor, and his mother studied economics. His grandfather was a famous engineer and university president back in China!

Growing up, Steven was curious about how things worked. He loved to take apart toys and put them back together. But he wasn't always a great student and once got a C in high school physics. Even brilliant scientists don't always start out on top!

Fun Fact: In eighth grade, Steven taught himself how to play tennis by reading a book. He also learned how to pole vault using bamboo poles from a local carpet store!

From Classroom to Laboratory

Despite that early C grade, Steven discovered he had a real talent for math and science. He went on to study physics at the University of Rochester, where he earned two degrees at once—one in math and one in physics.

Steven then continued his studies at the University of California, Berkeley. There, he earned his Ph.D. in physics in 1976. After finishing his Ph.D. work, Steven started working at Bell Labs, where many important scientific discoveries have been made.

But what exactly was his work? Steven figured out how to use lasers to cool and slow individual atoms. Now, you might be thinking, "Why would anyone want to slow atoms?" Well, by slowing atoms down by cooling them, scientists can study them much more closely. This helps us understand how the tiniest building blocks of our universe behave.

This discovery was so important that in 1997, Steven Chu was awarded the Nobel Prize in Physics, sharing it with two other scientists. He was only 49 years old at the time—quite young for a Nobel Prize winner.

From Lasers to Leadership

Steven became a professor at Stanford University, where he continued to do research on exciting areas of science, including ways to study tiny molecules like DNA in living cells. His work has helped scientists understand more about how our bodies work at the tiniest levels.

In 2004, Steven returned to the University of California and became the director of the Lawrence Berkeley National Laboratory. There, he led a team of scientists working on some of the world's biggest problems, like finding new sources of clean energy.

In 2009, something unexpected happened. President Barack Obama asked Steven Chu to become the U.S. Secretary of Energy. A really big deal! Steven became the first person to serve in the U.S. Cabinet after winning a Nobel Prize. He was also only the second Chinese American to be a Cabinet member.

As Secretary of Energy, Steven had a huge job. He was in charge of the country's energy policies and research to help America develop cleaner, more efficient ways to power our homes, cars, and businesses. He worked hard to promote clean energy sources like solar and wind power, believing that moving away from fossil fuels (like oil and coal) was essential to fight climate change and protect our planet.

Steven once said, "The Stone Age did not end because we ran out of stones; we transitioned to better solutions." In other words, we don't need to wait until we use up all our oil and coal before switching to cleaner energy. We can choose to make the change now, just like how people in the past chose to use better tools than stones.

Steven doesn't just point out problems—he works on solutions. He has some creative ideas for how we can combat climate change. For instance, he suggests painting roofs and roads white to reflect sunlight back into space. This simple change could have the same effect as taking every car in the world off the road for 11 years!

Overcoming Challenges

Being a scientist and a government leader isn't easy. Sometimes, Steven faced criticism for his ideas or decisions. When he suggested that we raise gasoline prices to encourage people to use less (like they do in

Europe), many Americans became upset. But Steven learned from this experience and later focused on finding ways to lower gas prices instead.

Despite challenges, Steven has always worked for what he thinks is right. He shows us that it's okay to change your mind when you learn new information, and that persistence is key when trying to solve big problems.

Inspiring Future Scientists

After serving as Secretary of Energy for four years, Steven returned to teaching at Stanford University. He continues to speak out about the dangers of climate change and the need for clean energy. He believes that scientific research can help us create a cleaner, more sustainable world for everyone.

He is also passionate about inspiring young people to pursue careers in science. He often encourages students to use their creativity and problem-solving skills to tackle the world's challenges.

What Ideas Influence Steven Chu?

Steven Chu started out as a curious kid. These ideas encourage his curiosity as an adult:

1. Never stop learning and keep learning new skills.

2. Big problems need creative solutions.

3. Don't be afraid to take on new challenges.

Think About It

Steven Chu continues to work on solving important problems and inspiring others to do the same. He shows us that science isn't just about working in a lab—it can be used to change the world. Maybe you'll be the next Steven Chu, making discoveries that change the world!

What problem in the world would you like to solve? How do you think you could step out of your comfort zone to work on it?

ROGER TSIEN

THE MAN WHO MADE MOLECULES GLOW
(1952-2016)

T he brilliant Asian American scientist, Roger Tsien, made peering into
living cells and tracking microscopic molecules within our bodies
jump from the stuff of science fiction to reality.

A Curious Child with a Bright Future

Roger Yonchien Tsien was born on February 1, 1952, in New York City.
His parents had come to America from China, bringing with them a rich
family history of scientists and engineers. His father was a mechanical
engineer, and he had uncles who were engineering professors at MIT.
Science and discovery ran in his blood.

As a child, Roger suffered from asthma, which meant he spent a lot of
time indoors. But he didn't let that stop him from exploring his passion

for science. Instead, he set up his very own chemistry lab in the basement of his family home.

When he was just 16 years old, he won first prize in a national science competition for a chemistry project. His project? It was all about how metals stick to a chemical called thiocyanate—pretty advanced stuff for a teenager!

Like Steven Chu, Roger wasn't always a straight-A student. And again, like Steven Chu, he once got a C in high school physics! Even brilliant scientists don't always start out perfect. What matters is their curiosity and hard work.

From Harvard to Cambridge: A Scientific Journey

Roger's brilliance led him to Harvard University, where he graduated with top honors in chemistry and physics. His college roommate once said, "It's probably not an exaggeration to say he's the smartest person I ever met."

After Harvard, Roger moved to England to study at the University of Cambridge. There, he earned his Ph.D. in physiology. Can you believe that he was only in his 20s when he was creating new tools to study how cells work?

The Rainbow Palette of Science

Roger's most famous work—his work with fluorescent proteins—won him the Nobel Prize in Chemistry in 2008. He and his team figured out how to make proteins in living cells glow with different colors!

Imagine a protein (a tiny machine in our cells) that glows when you shine a special light on it. That's a fluorescent protein. He took a protein that naturally glows green (found in jellyfish) and manipulated it to create proteins that glow in all the colors of the rainbow.

Roger and his team worked endlessly to create new versions of fluorescent proteins in all sorts of colors. They made proteins that glow green, yellow, blue, and even red! This might sound like just a fun art project, but it was actually a huge breakthrough for science.

These glowing proteins allow scientists to see inside living cells without harming them. With these colorful proteins, scientists could now track different parts of a cell at the same time. It's like being able to watch several TV shows on different channels all at once! This discovery has revolutionized how we study biology and medicine.

Now, Roger didn't discover the first fluorescent protein. That honor goes to another scientist named Osamu Shimomura, a scientist in Japan. But Roger took this discovery and made it incredibly useful for scientists all over the world.

Roger didn't stop at fluorescent proteins. He also created special dyes that change color when they detect certain chemicals in cells. One of his most famous inventions helps scientists see calcium in cells. Why is this important? Because calcium helps control many processes in our bodies, from how our hearts beat to how our brains think!

Overcoming Challenges

Roger's path wasn't always easy. As an Asian American in a field dominated by white scientists, he sometimes faced discrimination. But he never let that stop him. Instead, he let his work speak for itself.

He also faced health challenges later in life, including cancer and a stroke. But Roger's determination and love for science kept him going. He continued his research and made new discoveries even while facing these obstacles.

Impact on Science and Society

Roger's work has had an enormous impact on science and medicine. His glowing proteins are now used by researchers all over the world to study everything from how the brain works to how diseases spread in the body.

He also developed tools to help surgeons see cancer cells during operations, making it easier to remove tumors completely. And he worked on new ways to deliver medicines exactly where they're needed in the body.

What made Roger special wasn't just his scientific skills. It was his creativity. He approached science like an artist, always looking for new ways to bring color and light to the invisible world of cells.

Roger once said, "I'm sort of a tool builder. I build tools for other scientists to use." This shows how he saw his work—not just as a way to make discoveries but also as a way to help other scientists make their own discoveries.

Inspiring the Next Generation

Roger didn't keep his love of science to himself. He shared it with others, especially young people. He participated in science festivals and often spoke to students about the excitement of scientific discovery.

His work continues to inspire scientists, especially young Asian Americans, to pursue careers in science and innovation.

What Ideas Influenced Roger Tsien?

Roger Tsien passed away in 2016, but his work continues to light up laboratories around the world. Every day, scientists use the tools he created to make new discoveries about how our bodies work and how to treat diseases.

Like his work, the ideas that influenced Roger were powerful:

1. Follow your passion and don't let go.

2. Think creatively. Think outside of the box.

3. Do your best work and let it speak for itself.

4. Share your talents and discoveries.

Think About It

Roger Tsien's story reminds us that science isn't just about memorizing facts—it's about exploring, creating, and finding colorful ways to understand our world.

So go ahead, let your curiosity glow! When you do, what will you light up?

KALPANA CHAWLA

REACHING FOR THE STARS: FIRST INDIAN-AMERICAN WOMAN IN SPACE (1962-2003)

Gazing at the night sky, many of us dream of floating among the stars. For Kalpana Chawla, this dream became a reality. As the first Indian American woman to fly in space, Kalpana broke barriers and inspired millions around the world.

An Inquisitive Mind Takes Flight

Kalpana Chawla was born the youngest of four children on March 17, 1962, in Karnal, a city in the Indian state of Haryana. As a child, she loved to watch planes soar through the sky and often visited local flying clubs with her father. She felt excitement as she watched those planes take off, wondering if she, too, could one day fly high above the clouds. But Kalpana's journey to the stars began in the classroom.

She was an excellent student, especially in science and math. She wasn't content to just learn from books—she wanted to understand how things worked and asked questions. This curiosity would serve her well in her future career as an astronaut and aerospace engineer.

Breaking Traditions and Pursuing Dreams

In India during Kalpana's youth, it wasn't common for girls to pursue careers in science and engineering. But Kalpana was determined to follow her passion. After finishing high school at Tagore Baal Niketan Senior Secondary School in Karnal, she earned a bachelor's degree in Aeronautical Engineering from Punjab Engineering College in 1982. This was unusual for a young woman in India at that time. But Kalpana wasn't afraid to be different. This was just the beginning of her educational journey.

Kalpana knew that to achieve her dreams, she needed to learn even more. In 1982, at the age of 20, she made a bold move. She left India and traveled to the United States to continue her studies.

In America, Kalpana earned not one but two master's degrees in aerospace engineering—one from the University of Texas at Arlington and the other from the University of Colorado Boulder. She then went on to complete a Ph.D in the same field at the University of Colorado. She also became a certified flight instructor and held commercial pilot licenses for airplanes, seaplanes, and gliders.

After finishing her academic studies, Kalpana started working for NASA at the Ames Research Center. Her job involved studying how air moves around aircraft, which is crucial knowledge for designing better planes and spacecraft. From there she continued aerodynamics research in the private sector.

Reaching for the Stars

After becoming a U.S. citizen in 1991, Kalpana applied to join the NASA Astronaut Corps. In 1994, she was selected to become an astronaut candidate. This was a highly competitive process—thousands of people apply, but only a few are chosen. Kalpana's exceptional skills and dedication had paid off. In 1995, she was assigned to the 15th Group of Astronauts for astronaut training.

On November 19, 1997, Kalpana achieved a historic milestone. She became the first Indian American woman to fly in space as part of the Space Shuttle Columbia mission STS-87. During this 16-day mission, Kalpana traveled an incredible 6.5 million miles and orbited Earth 252 times! Her main job was to operate the shuttle's robotic arm to deploy the Spartan Satellite and to conduct scientific experiments.

While floating onboard in the weightlessness of space, Kalpana shared a profound thought: "You are just your intelligence."

This quote reminds us that our minds and our determination are what truly define us, not our appearance or where we come from.

Challenges and Perseverance

As a woman in a male-dominated field, Kalpana often faced skepticism and doubt. But she never let these challenges stop her. Instead, she used them as motivation to work even harder and prove herself.

During her first space mission—mission STS-87—Kalpana faced a significant challenge when a satellite she was responsible for deploying malfunctioned. This led to a NASA investigation, but Kalpana was eventually cleared of any wrongdoing. Instead of letting this setback discourage her, she used it as an opportunity to learn and improve.

A Tragic End and a Lasting Legacy

Kalpana's passion for space exploration didn't end with her first mission. In 2003, she returned to space aboard Columbia for the STS-107 mission. This time, she and her fellow crew members conducted nearly 80 scientific experiments, studying everything from Earth science to technology development.

Tragically, on February 1, 2003, as the shuttle was returning to Earth, it broke apart, claiming the lives of Kalpana and her six crewmates.

While Kalpana's life was cut short, her impact continues to inspire people around the world, especially young Asian Americans and girls interested in science and space exploration. With hard work, determination, and courage, we can achieve even our most ambitious dreams.

Inspiring Future Generations

Kalpana's legacy lives on in many ways. Numerous schools, universities, and institutions have been named in her honor. The Kalpana Chawla Award was created to recognize young women scientists in India and a mountain peak in the Columbia Hills on Mars is named "Chawla Hill" in her honor. Even a star in the night sky bears her name—asteroid 51826 Kalpana Chawla.

What Ideas Influenced Kalpana Chawla?

Kalpana means "imagination" in Sanskrit—a fitting name for someone who imagined herself among the stars ... and who believed that "you are just your intelligence."

Perhaps Kalpana followed these ideas:

1. Learn, learn, and learn even more.

2. Set a goal and go for it.

3. Be brave.

4. Never give up.

Think About It

Kalpana Chawla's journey from India to the U.S. to the vastness of space shows us that there are no limits to what we can achieve if we dare to dream big, work hard, and persevere. Her story inspires people around the world to reach for the stars—both literally and figuratively.

Do you have any idea what your story will be?

JERRY YANG

FROM IMMIGRANT TO INTERNET PIONEER
(1968-)

J erry Yang, an Asian American entrepreneur, transformed from a young immigrant who barely spoke English into the co-founder of one of the world's most famous internet companies, Yahoo! His journey is an amazing tale of determination, innovation, and success.

A New Start in America

Jerry Yang was born in Taipei, Taiwan, on November 6, 1968. His father passed away when he was only two years old, so when Jerry was ten, his mother bravely moved the family to San Jose, California, hoping for better opportunities.

Jerry says he only knew one English word when he came to America: "shoe." But he was determined to learn. He worked hard and became fluent in English in just three years. This early experience taught Jerry that with dedication and effort, you can overcome seemingly impossible obstacles.

From Stanford to Silicon Valley

Jerry's love for learning didn't stop with English. He excelled in school, especially in math and science. After graduating from high school, he went to Stanford University, one of the best colleges in the country. There, he studied electrical engineering and earned two degrees in only four years!

It was at Stanford that Jerry met David Filo, who would become his friend and business partner; a union that would change the internet forever.

In 1994, while still students at Stanford, Jerry and David had an idea. They created a website that was like a directory for the internet, which was still new and difficult to navigate. They called their search engine, "Jerry and David's Guide to the World Wide Web."

The guide was a directory of other websites, helping people find what they were looking for online. As more and more people started using the internet, their website became very popular. They needed a catchier name so chose "Yahoo!" which stands for "Yet Another Hierarchical Officious Oracle." It's quite a mouthful, isn't it? But "Yahoo!" was fun to say and easy to remember. It soon grew into one of the most visited sites on the internet.

Building an Internet Giant

Jerry and David's timing was perfect. They started Yahoo! just as the internet was becoming a big part of people's lives. Within a year, Yahoo! was getting 100,000 visitors every day! In 1995, Jerry and David got their first big investment of $2 million. They hired Tim Koogle as CEO, and Jerry and David became "Chief Yahoos."

The company kept growing, and in 1996, when Jerry was only 27 years old, Yahoo! became a public company with 49 employees. This meant any member of the public could buy a piece of the company. "Going public" made Jerry *very* rich.

Jerry's role at Yahoo! changed over the years. He was the co-founder, but he also served as CEO from 2007 to 2009. Jerry made some important decisions that helped the company grow and change over the years. Under his leadership, Yahoo! grew from a search engine to offer email, news, and many other services that millions of people use every day.

One of Jerry's smartest moves was investing in a Chinese company called Alibaba in 2005. Yahoo! bought 40% of Alibaba for $1 billion. This turned out to be an incredibly good decision. When Yahoo! sold some of its Alibaba shares years later, it made billions of dollars!

Beyond Yahoo!

After leaving Yahoo! in 2012, Jerry didn't stop working. He started a new company called AME Cloud Ventures. This company invests in new technology startups, helping other entrepreneurs turn their ideas into successful businesses.

Jerry also uses his success to give back to the community. In 2007, he and his wife, Akiko Yamazaki, donated $75 million to Stanford University. Part of this money was used to build a new environmentally friendly building for research and teaching.

Challenges and Tough Decisions

Being a business leader isn't always easy, and Jerry faced some difficult challenges. In 2008, Microsoft offered to buy Yahoo! for $44.6 billion. That's more money than most of us can imagine. But Jerry believed in Yahoo!'s potential and didn't want to sell. This decision is still controversial today.

Jerry also had to make tough choices when doing business in other countries. In 2007, he apologized to the families of Chinese journalists who were arrested after Yahoo! shared their information with the Chinese government. Jerry learned from this experience and created a fund to help protect human rights online.

Impact on the Asian American Community and His Lasting Impact on the Technology World

Jerry Yang's success shows that immigrants can achieve great things in the United States through hard work and innovation. He once said, "There is no overnight success. You have to be patient, and you have to be persistent."

Jerry and Akiko Yamazaki are also passionate about art. They have a large collection of Chinese calligraphy, which they've shared with museums so that others can enjoy and learn from it. In 2017, they donated $25 million to the Asian Art Museum in San Francisco—the largest donation in the museum's history! In 2021, Jerry helped start The Asian American Foundation, which works to stop racism against Asian Americans and support the Asian American and Pacific Islander community.

Even though Jerry left Yahoo! in 2012, his impact on the internet and technology world continues. He now invests in and mentors new technology startups, like Zoom, helping the next generation of entrepreneurs bring their ideas to life.

What Ideas Influence Jerry Yang?

Jerry Yang continues to see potential in good ideas. Whether for business or for philanthropy, Jerry is influenced by core ideas like these:

1. Think big and think positive.

2. Take risks.

3. Work hard and be persistent.

4. Mentor people and their ideas.

5. Share your passions, including the arts!

Think About It

Remember, every big success starts with a single step. Who knows? Maybe you'll be the next Jerry Yang, creating something that changes the world!

What big ideas do you have? How could you use technology or the internet to make the world a better place?

ACTIVISM & POLITICS

VOICES FOR CHANGE AND PROGRESS

DALIP SINGH SAUND

THE FIRST ASIAN AMERICAN IN CONGRESS (1899-1973)

From a small village in India to a Ph.D. in math to being a farmer, a judge, and a Congressman in Washington D.C., Dalip Singh Saund's life embodies the power of big dreams and unwavering determination.

Early Life and Journey to America

Dalip Singh Saund was born on September 20, 1899, in Chajulwadi, India. At that time life wasn't easy for young Dalip. India was still under British rule, and his father passed away when he was just ten years old. But even as a child, Dalip showed a desire to make a difference in the world.

As a student at the University of Punjab, Dalip became involved in the Indian independence movement of Mohandas Gandhi, dreaming of a free India. He graduated with a degree in mathematics in 1919 and, at the age of 21, made a big decision. He set sail for America with money borrowed from his brother and arrived in California on September 27. He was ready to study at the University of California, Berkeley.

From Student to Farmer

When Dalip arrived in America, he intended to learn about food preservation. But his curious mind led him to explore much more. He studied hard and excelled, earning a master's degree in 1922 and a Ph.D. in 1924. But even with his impressive education, Dalip faced racism as an immigrant in America.

After finishing his studies, Dalip could have become a professor or a scientist. But he chose a different path. In 1925, he became a farmer in California's Imperial Valley. Why would someone with a Ph.D. become a farmer?

Fighting for Citizenship and Justice

Dalip saw an opportunity to build a good life in America. While working as a melon and fertilizer farmer, he became involved in local politics. At that time, people from India weren't allowed to become U.S. citizens. Despite his education and contributions to his community, Dalip couldn't vote or hold public office.

He organized the Indian Association of America and worked tirelessly to change the laws that prevented Indians from becoming citizens. The Luce-Celler Act was passed in 1946, finally allowing Indians to apply for citizenship.

On December 16, 1949, Dalip Singh Saund proudly became a United States citizen. He wanted to make a difference in his community and serve his chosen country.

From Farmer to Judge

Dalip first ran for the position of Justice of the Peace in 1950, but while he won the election, he wasn't allowed to take the job because he hadn't been a citizen long enough. Did this setback stop him? Not at all! He ran again in 1952 and won, becoming the Justice of the Peace for Westmoreland, California … and one of the first Indian Americans to hold public office in the United States.

A Historic Election

In 1956, Dalip ran for the United States House of Representatives. Some people questioned whether he should be allowed to run because of his roots. But Dalip persevered, winning both the Democratic Party nomination and the general election.

When Dalip Singh Saund was sworn in as a member of the 85th United States Congress on January 3, 1957, he made history. He was the first Asian American, first Indian American, and first Sikh to serve in the U.S. Congress.

Making a Difference in Congress

During his time in Congress, Dalip worked hard to represent his district and to be a voice for Asian Americans and other minorities. He served on important committees, including a subcommittee of the House Foreign Affairs Committee. He used his unique background to help improve America's relationships with other countries, especially in Asia.

In 1957, Dalip traveled to represent the U.S. on a tour of several Asian countries. He even met with world leaders like Prime Minister Jawaharlal

Nehru of India and President Sukarno of Indonesia. He used these meetings to help Americans and Asians understand each other better.

Dalip wasn't afraid to speak his mind, even when it meant criticizing U.S. policies. In 1957, he said, "We cannot win the friendship of the teeming masses of Asia by buying kings and protecting oil." He believed that America needed to focus on helping the people of other countries, not just their leaders. He believed this was the best way to make friends around the world.

Dalip served in Congress for three terms, from 1957 to 1963. His career was cut short by a stroke he suffered in 1962. He won the Democratic nomination from his hospital bed but lost the general election and was unable to return to Congress.

Legacy and Inspiration for Today's Youth

Today, there are many more Asian Americans serving in Congress and other levels of government, but Dalip Singh Saund was the pioneer who showed it was possible.

His legacy lives on in every Asian American elected official, and his life story inspires all Americans, but especially Asian American youth. He showed that with hard work, determination, and a commitment to public service, anyone can make a difference in their community and their country.

Dalip once said, "There is no room in the United States of America for second-class citizenship."

This powerful statement reminds us that everyone deserves equal rights and opportunities, regardless of their background.

What Ideas Influenced Dalip Sing Saund?

"The great United States of America was built by people from all over the world." Dalip's quote reminds us that America's strength comes from its diversity. His other ideas can influence young Americans today:

1. Never stop learning or trying new things.

2. Stand up for what's right.

3. Represent your community.

4. Don't let others tell you what you can't do.

Think About It

Like Dalip Singh Saund you have the power to make history and inspire others. All it takes is courage, hard work, and the belief that anything is possible in America.

What barriers would you like to break? What positive changes could you make in your community or even in the world?

GRACE LEE BOGGS

A LIFELONG REVOLUTIONARY (1915-2015)

G race Lee Boggs embodied the true spirit of a revolutionary. This remarkable Chinese American woman dedicated her entire 100-year
life to fighting for justice and creating positive change in her community.

Early Life and Education

Grace Lee was born on June 27, 1915, in Providence, Rhode Island, where
her parents—recent immigrants from China—owned a Chinese restaurant. When Grace was 8 years old, her family moved to Queens, New York
City, where they were the only Chinese people in their neighborhood.

As a young girl, Grace felt caught between the worlds of her Chinese
heritage, her American identity, and her feminism. She later recalled, "I
didn't think of myself as Chinese because the Chinese American movement hadn't emerged, and I didn't think of myself as a woman because

the women's movement hadn't emerged." The quote shows how Grace felt confused about who she was because there weren't yet groups or movements to help her understand what it meant to be Chinese American or a woman.

Despite these challenges, at just 16 years old, Grace won a scholarship to attend Barnard College, one of the best women's colleges in the country. There, she discovered a passion for philosophy—the study of big ideas about life, knowledge, and how we should treat each other. She was one of only three students of color in her class. After graduating in 1935, Grace went on to earn her Ph.D. in philosophy from Bryn Mawr College in 1940. This was an incredible achievement at that time, especially for a woman of color.

Facing Discrimination and Finding Her Path

Despite having a Ph.D. from a prestigious school, Grace couldn't find a teaching job as a professor. Many universities and employers in the 1940s wouldn't hire women, especially women of color. Grace recalled that "Even department stores would say, 'We don't hire Orientals.'"

Finally, Grace got a job working in the philosophy library at the University of Chicago. The pay was very low, and she couldn't afford to rent an apartment, so she lived for free in a basement filled with rats!

It was during this difficult time that one day, she saw a group of African Americans protesting the poor living conditions in their neighborhood. Their struggles were like her own. Grace's eyes opened to the connections between different communities facing injustice and discrimination.

Grace soon began fighting for the rights of workers and tenants. She joined socialist groups and wrote about social and political issues. Her true calling was not in teaching in a classroom but in working directly with people to create positive change in their lives.

A Life of Activism in Detroit

In the 1950s, Grace moved to Detroit, Michigan, and met James Boggs, an African American auto worker and activist. They married in 1953 and became an unstoppable team, working together for over 40 years until James passed away in 1993.

Grace and James Boggs became two of Detroit's most famous activists. They fought for civil rights—to end racial discrimination and promote equality for all people, workers' rights—for fair treatment and better conditions for factory workers, education—for learning and free community-based education, as well as environmental Justice—where they saw the connection between social issues and caring for the planet.

Grace strongly believed in the power of community organizing and grassroots movements. She and James helped start many local organizations, and their home was always open to other activists and thinkers. Even Malcolm X stayed with them when he visited Detroit!

Grace and James didn't just talk about these issues—they took action. They wrote books, organized protests, and started community programs. They weren't afraid to challenge powerful people or unpopular ideas if they believed it was the right thing to do.

Evolving Ideas on Revolution

As she grew older, Grace's ideas about how to create change evolved. In her younger years, she believed in the need for a dramatic revolution. In the 1960s and 1970s, she was involved in many protests and demonstrations. But Grace came to see that lasting change required more than just protests or quick fixes and began to focus more on building strong communities from the ground up.

Grace began to concentrate on what she called "visionary organizing"—bringing people together to imagine and build the kind of society they wanted to live in. She encouraged people to be "solutionaries" rather than just revolutionaries. "We are the leaders we've been looking for," Grace would say.

In 1992, when she was 77 years old, Grace helped start a program called Detroit Summer. Young people came together to work on community projects like planting gardens, painting murals, and fixing up abandoned buildings. Grace believed that by working together on positive projects, people could create the kind of world they wanted to live in.

Inspiring Future Generations

Even into her 90s and nearing 100, Grace Lee Boggs never stopped working for change. She continued writing, speaking, and mentoring young activists until the very end of her long life. In 2011, at the age of 95, she published a book called *The Next American Revolution: Sustainable Activism for the Twenty-First Century.*

In 2013, a documentary film called *American Revolutionary: The Evolution of Grace Lee Boggs* introduced Grace's amazing life story to new audiences. The James and Grace Lee Boggs School, which opened in Detroit that same year, carries on her vision of community-based education.

What Ideas Influenced Grace Lee Boggs?

Grace passed away on October 5, 2015, at the age of 100. But her legacy lives on through the many people she inspired with ideas like these:

1. Keep growing and evolving. Be open to new ideas. Reimagine what's possible.

2. Building connections across different communities makes us stronger.

3. Think globally, act locally.

4. Age is just a number—You're never too young or too old to make a difference in the world.

Think About It

Remember Grace's words: "You cannot change any society unless you take responsibility for it, unless you see yourself as belonging to it and responsible for changing it."

What problems do you see in your community? How do you think you could work as a "solutionary" with others to make positive changes?

DANIEL INOUYE

FROM WAR HERO TO PIONEERING SENATOR
(1924-2012)

D aniel Inouye was a true American hero. As the first Japanese American to serve in the U.S. Congress and the highest-ranking Asian American politician in U.S. history for many years, Inouye's path from a young soldier to a respected senator is both inspiring and extraordinary.

Early Life and Background

Daniel Ken Inouye was born on September 7, 1924, in Honolulu, Hawaii, before Hawaii was a state. His father was a jeweler who had immigrated to Hawaii from Japan, and Daniel's mother's parents were also Japanese immigrants. This makes Daniel a *Nisei* (second-generation Japanese American) through his father and a *Sansei* (third-generation) through his mother. Growing up in Hawaii, Daniel experienced a mix of cultures and the value of diversity from an early age.

As a teenager, Daniel's life changed dramatically when he witnessed the attack by the Japanese Navy on Pearl Harbor on December 7, 1941. At just 17 years old, he rushed to help tend to the wounded as a medical volunteer. The attack brought the United States into World War II and also had a profound impact on Daniel's life and the lives of many Japanese Americans.

A True War Hero

After the Pearl Harbor attack, Japanese Americans faced intense discrimination. Many families had their homes and assets taken away and were sent to internment camps in the mainland United States. Although Hawaii's Japanese American population wasn't widely interned, they still faced suspicion and prejudice.

Despite this, Daniel and many other young Japanese Americans wanted to prove their loyalty to the United States. When the U.S. government finally allowed Japanese Americans to enlist in 1943, Daniel immediately volunteered. He joined the 442nd Regimental Combat Team, a unit made up entirely of Japanese American soldiers, fighting bravely for a country that didn't always treat them fairly. This group became one of the most decorated units in U.S. military history.

During a fierce battle in Italy in 1945, Daniel displayed incredible bravery. After being shot in the stomach he continued to lead his platoon against enemy positions. Then, horrifyingly, a grenade blast took off most of his right arm. But instead of retreating, Daniel pried the live grenade he was holding from his now-useless right hand and threw it at the enemy with his left hand. He fought until he fell unconscious.

For his extraordinary courage, Daniel was awarded the Distinguished Service Cross, which was later upgraded to the Medal of Honor, the nation's highest military award.

Major Achievements and Contributions

After the war, Daniel had to give up his dream of becoming a surgeon due to his arm, but he found a new way to serve his country. He decided to study law and enter politics to make a difference for all Americans, especially those facing discrimination.

Daniel enrolled at the University of Hawaii at Mānoa to study government and economics. After graduating in 1950, he moved with his wife to Washington D.C. so he could continue his studies at George Washington University Law School. He earned his J.D. in two years and moved back to Hawaii in 1952. There he got his license to practice law and worked as a public prosecutor for several years while slowly building his career in politics.

In 1959, when Hawaii became a state, Daniel Inouye was elected as its first full member in the U.S. House of Representatives. Just three years later, he won election to the U.S. Senate, where he would serve for nearly 50 years until his death in 2012.

During his time in Congress, Daniel was a strong supporter of civil rights and equality for all Americans and worked to improve educational opportunities, especially for disadvantaged students. As a veteran himself, he was a powerful advocate for those who served in the military, and as a Hawaiian, he fought to preserve Native Hawaiian culture and rights.

Daniel's integrity and fairness earned him respect from both Democrats and Republicans.

A Voice for Asian Americans and Pacific Islanders

Daniel, never forgetting his own history, became a powerful voice for Asian Americans and Pacific Islanders. He supported legislation that provided reparations to Japanese Americans interned during World War II, established Asian Pacific American Heritage Month, and created the

Asian American and Native American Pacific Islander-Serving Institutions Program to support colleges serving these communities.

For decades, Daniel's presence in the Senate helped ensure that the voices and concerns of Asian Americans were heard at the national level.

Impact on the Asian American Community and Broader Society

But his impact went beyond just the Asian American community. He worked for the benefit of *all* Americans, regardless of their background.

He once said, "America is not a country where only the white man can be president. Any boy or girl can dream of becoming the president of the United States."

A Legacy of Inspiration

Daniel Inouye passed away on December 17, 2012, at the age of 88. His last word was reportedly "Aloha," a fitting farewell for a man who dedicated his life to serving Hawaii and the entire United States.

Daniel Inouye's influence continues to be felt. Buildings, institutions, and even a Navy ship have been named in his honor. The Daniel K. Inouye International Airport in Honolulu is perhaps the most visible tribute to his legacy. But most importantly, Daniel's career showed young Asian Americans that they, too, could aspire to the highest levels of government.

What Ideas Influenced Daniel Inouye?

Daniel once said, "America is not a country where only certain groups are entitled to equality. America is for everyone." This belief shaped his vision for leadership.

These ideas might have done the same:

1. Show courage in the face of challenge.

2. Stay determined and work until the job is done.

3. Serve others, especially those who need help.

4. Anyone can overcome great obstacles and make a positive difference in the world.

Think About It

You don't have to be a senator or a war hero to make a difference. Every day, you have the opportunity to show courage, learn, serve others, and break down barriers.

Do you have any ideas of how you can show your courage? What would inspire you to do that?

PATSY TAKEMOTO MINK

BREAKING BARRIERS AND FIGHTING FOR EQUALITY (1927-2002)

P atsy Takemoto Mink was an individual with the courage to stand up for what's right. As the first woman of color and the first Asian-American woman elected to the United States Congress, Patsy Mink broke barriers and fought for equality throughout her life.

Early Life and Challenges

Born on December 6, 1927, on the island of Maui in Hawaii, Patsy Takemoto grew up on a sugar plantation where her family worked. Her grandparents had come to Hawaii from Japan, making Patsy a third-generation Japanese American (a *Sansei*).

Patsy was a bright and curious child. She loved learning and school, but even as a young girl, she noticed that some people were treated differently because of how they looked or where their families came from. A natural leader, she vowed to change things when she grew up.

When she applied to medical school after college, Patsy faced her first big challenge. She was rejected by 12 different schools because she was a woman! This unfair treatment made her angry and more determined to fight against discrimination. She would become a lawyer.

Patsy enrolled in the University of Chicago Law School, where she was one of only two female students. There, she met her husband, John Mink, and married him in 1951. After graduating that same year, Patsy faced another challenge: no law firm would hire her because she was a married woman with a child. So ... she started her own law practice! In 1953, she became the first Japanese American woman to practice law in Hawaii.

Fighting for Change in Politics

Patsy realized that to make big changes, she needed to get involved in politics. In 1956, she was elected to the Hawaiian territorial legislature, becoming the first Japanese American woman to serve there. In 1964, her history-making continued, and Patsy Mink became the first woman of color elected to the United States Congress!

In Congress, Patsy created laws that improved life for everyone, especially women and minorities. She believed in education as the key to success and fought to make sure all Americans had access to good schools and colleges. One of her laws, Title IX, says no one can be discriminated against in education because of their gender. Before this law, many schools and colleges treated boys and girls differently, some not allowing girls to play sports or take certain classes.

Thanks to Title IX, girls and boys now have equal opportunities in school. This means girls can play sports, take science classes, or do anything else they're interested in, just like boys can. The law has had a huge impact on education and sports in America.

Patsy wanted to make sure that future generations wouldn't have to face the same discriminatory challenges she did.

Overcoming Obstacles

Throughout her career, Patsy faced many challenges. She once said, "It is easy enough to vote right and be consistently with the majority. But it is more often more important to be ahead of the majority and this means being willing to cut the first furrow in the ground and stand alone for a while if necessary."

In other words, Patsy believed that doing the right thing was more important than being popular. She wasn't afraid to stand up for what she believed in, even if she had to stand alone.

Impact on the Asian American Community and Beyond

Patsy Mink's work in Congress didn't just help women and girls—it helped people of all backgrounds. She fought for civil rights, worked to protect the environment, and tried to end the Vietnam War. For Asian Americans, seeing Patsy in Congress was inspiring. She helped create the Congressional Asian Pacific American Caucus, a group of politicians who work together on issues important to Asian Americans and Pacific Islanders. This group still exists today and continues to fight for equality and representation.

In 1972, Patsy even ran for President of the United States! While she didn't win, she became the first Asian-American woman to run for this high office.

Patsy's dedication to public service lasted her entire life. She served in Congress for a total of 24 years, fighting for the rights of women, minorities, and all Americans until her passing in 2002.

Legacy and Continued Influence

Patsy Mink's legacy lives on. The Title IX law she helped create was renamed the "Patsy T. Mink Equal Opportunity in Education Act" in her honor. Thanks to this law, millions of girls and women have had the chance to play sports, study science and math, and pursue their dreams in ways that weren't possible before.

In 2014, President Barack Obama posthumously awarded Patsy the Presidential Medal of Freedom, the highest civilian honor in the United States. He said, "Patsy was a passionate advocate for opportunity and equality who touched countless lives."

Every time a woman or person of color enters high-level government, and every time a girl plays on a sports team at school, or a woman becomes a scientist or engineer, they're building on the foundation that Patsy Mink helped create.

What Ideas Influenced Patsy Takemoto Mink?

Patsy Takemoto Mink's life shows us that one person really can make a difference. She faced many obstacles but wasn't afraid to be the first or to stand alone when fighting for important causes.

Perhaps these are a few of the ideas that influenced Patsy Mink as she followed her dream to create a fairer world:

1. Determine what you want to accomplish and stay on it.

2. Fighting discrimination is good for all Americans.

3. Persevere, even if you do it alone.

4. Never give up on your dreams.

Think About It

Today, we can see the results of Patsy's hard work all around us. Girls play on sports teams, take advanced science classes, and dream of becoming anything they want to be—even President of the United States!

Do you have a dream for your future? If so, what would you want to do today to make progress toward achieving it?

KAMALA HARRIS

MADAM VEEP -- FROM OAKLAND TO THE OVAL OFFICE (1964-)

The 49th Vice President of the United States, Kamala Harris, has lived a life full of "firsts." The daughter of immigrants, she has become one of the most powerful and inspiring leaders in America!

A Childhood of Diversity and Dreams

Kamala Devi Harris was born on October 20, 1964, in Oakland, California. Her mother, Shyamala Gopalan, was a brilliant scientist from India who studied breast cancer. Her father, Donald Harris, came from Jamaica and became an economics professor. Growing up, Kamala was surrounded by a mix of cultures that would shape her worldview.

Fun Fact: Kamala's first name means "lotus flower" in Sanskrit, and her middle name, Devi, means "goddess."

As a child, Kamala lived in a diverse neighborhood in Berkeley, California. She and her younger sister, Maya, were part of a school integration program that bussed them to a school outside of their own neighborhood.* This early experience taught Kamala about the importance of equality and fairness.

Kamala's parents divorced when she was seven, and her mother raised her and Maya as a single parent. They moved around a bit, even living in Montreal, Canada, for a few years! Through it all, Kamala's mother instilled in her daughters a strong sense of pride in their heritage and a belief that they could achieve anything they set their minds to.

*This practice called "bussing" started in the 1950s to create more diversity in schools. It involved taking students by bus to schools outside their neighborhoods, mixing kids of different races and backgrounds. The goal was to end school segregation and give all students equal learning opportunities.

Finding Her Voice and Purpose

As Kamala grew older, she became more aware of injustice in the world and wanted to make a difference. Inspired by civil rights leaders like Thurgood Marshall, she decided to become a lawyer. After high school, Kamala attended Howard University, a historically Black college in Washington, D.C. There, she joined a sorority, led the debate team, and interned for a California senator. These experiences helped her develop leadership skills and a passion for public service.

After earning her law degree in San Francisco, Kamala began her career as a prosecutor in Oakland. She worked hard to protect victims of crime, especially children and families.

As she rose in her career, Kamala never forgot her roots or the values her mother taught her. She is proud of her mixed heritage and uses her experiences to connect with many different people.

Breaking Barriers in California

Kamala's determination and skill as a lawyer led her to new challenges. In 2003, she was elected as the District Attorney of San Francisco. This made her the first woman, first African American, and first South Asian American to hold this important position in the city!

In 2010, she became the Attorney General of California—the top lawyer for the entire state. Once again, she broke barriers and was the first woman and first person of color to have this job. As Attorney General, Kamala fought for civil rights, to protect the environment, and against unfair practices of big banks.

A Voice in the Senate

In 2016, Kamala became the second Black woman and first South Asian American ever to win a seat in the U.S. Senate.

As a senator, Kamala worked on important issues like healthcare, immigration reform, and criminal justice. She became known for asking tough questions and standing up for what she believed in. She wasn't afraid to challenge powerful people, even during important hearings watched by millions of Americans on TV.

Making History as Vice President

In 2019, Kamala ran for President of the United States. Although she didn't win the Democratic nomination, she caught the attention of Joe Biden, who did win the nomination. He chose Kamala to be his running mate, and together, they won the 2020 election.

On January 20, 2021, Kamala Harris was sworn in as the 49th Vice President of the United States. This historic moment marked many firsts:

- First woman Vice President

- First African American Vice President

- First Asian American Vice President

- Highest-ranking female elected official in U.S. history

As Vice President, Kamala has taken on important responsibilities like working on immigration issues and promoting voting rights. She also plays a crucial role in the Senate, where she can cast tie-breaking votes when senators are evenly split on an issue.

Inspiring the Next Generation

Throughout her career, Kamala Harris has often been the "first" person like her in a room. But she doesn't want to be the last. Kamala once said, "My mother would look at me and she'd say, 'Kamala, you may be the first to do many things, but make sure you're not the last.'"

Kamala works hard to inspire young people to work through their fears, dream big, and pursue their goals.

What Ideas Influence Kamala Harris?

Kamala's inspirational story shows us the kinds of ideas that influence her. Here are a few:

1. Embrace your unique background.

2. Stand up for what you believe in.

3. Be willing to be first, even when the journey gets hard.

4. Keep learning and growing and taking on new challenges.

5. Remember where you came from and the people and community that supported you.

What's Next for Kamala Harris?

In late July of 2024, President Biden announced his withdrawal from the reelection race and endorsed Vice President Harris as his successor. She had less than four months to ramp up her campaign for the election in November. She lifted up the spirits of many people in the country with her positive messages of hope for the future, while inviting everyone -- even those who didn't agree with her -- to join her in the fight for decency, compassion, and democracy itself.

Even though she didn't win in the end, she showed real class by accepting the results and helping make sure the next president could take over smoothly. Regardless of her loss, and whatever challenge she may take on next, Kamala's story will continue to inspire people around the world to dream big and work hard to achieve their goals.

Think About It

Kamala Harris's journey from a little girl bussed in Oakland, California, to the White House is a powerful reminder that in America, anything is possible with hard work, determination, and a commitment to making the world a better place.

What challenges do you think Kamala Harris faced as she broke so many barriers in her career? What's a barrier in your own life that you'd like to break? How might Kamala's story inspire you to do that?

What will your story be?

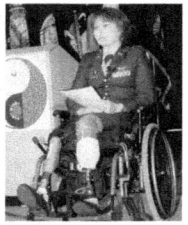

TAMMY DUCKWORTH

FROM WARRIOR TO SENATOR (1968-)

T ammy Duckworth is a true American hero. As the first Thai American woman elected to Congress and the first female double amputee in the U.S. Senate, Tammy's story is one of courage, perseverance, and unwavering service to others.

A Childhood Across Cultures

Ladda Tammy Duckworth was born on March 12, 1968, in Bangkok, Thailand. Her father was an American veteran who worked with refugees, and her mother was Thai Chinese. Tammy lived in Thailand, Indonesia, and Singapore before moving to Hawaii when she was 16. This gave her a unique perspective on the world and taught her to adapt to new situations quickly.

From Girl Scout to Soldier

Even though Tammy's family sometimes struggled financially and even had to rely on food stamps, as a teenager in Hawaii, Tammy was determined to make the most of the opportunities she had. She joined the Girl Scouts and earned their highest honor, the Gold Award.

After high school, she went to the University of Hawaii at Mãnoa, George Washington University in Washington, D.C., and Capella University, eventually earning three degrees, including a Ph.D. in human services. But Tammy wanted to do more than just study—she wanted to serve her country.

In 1990, Tammy joined the Army Reserve Officers' Training Corps (ROTC). She became a commissioned officer in 1992 and chose to fly helicopters because it was one of the few combat jobs open to women at the time.

A Life-Changing Mission

Tammy became a helicopter pilot in the Army National Guard. She loved flying and was proud to serve her country. In 2004, Tammy was deployed to Iraq. On November 12, her Black Hawk helicopter was hit by a rocket-propelled grenade fired by Iraqi insurgents. The explosion caused Tammy to lose both of her legs and severely damaged her right arm. Despite being dangerously injured, she courageously helped land the helicopter, saving the lives of her crew.

Tammy spent the next year recovering at Walter Reed Army Medical Center in Bethesda, Maryland. Her road to recovery was long and challenging. She faced countless surgeries and grueling physical therapy sessions. She had to learn how to walk again using prosthetic legs. But she didn't just learn to walk... she learned to run, swim, and even surf!

Tammy said, "You can sit there and feel sorry for yourself, or you can get up and make the best of the situation and keep serving."

Through it all, Tammy found a new purpose. She decided to use her experience to help other veterans and fight for those who couldn't fight for themselves.

From Battlefield to Capitol Hill

After recovering from her injuries, Tammy found a new way to serve her country. She decided to enter politics and ran for Congress in 2006. Although she didn't win that first race, she didn't let it discourage her. She went on to serve as Director of the Illinois Department of Veterans Affairs and later as an Assistant Secretary in the U.S. Department of Veterans Affairs.

In 2012, she was elected to the U.S. House of Representatives, becoming the first Thai American woman and the first woman with a disability to serve in Congress. But Tammy didn't stop there. In 2016, she was elected to the U.S. Senate, becoming only the second Asian American woman ever to serve in that role.

Breaking Barriers and Inspiring Others

Throughout her career, Tammy has continued to break barriers. In 2018, she became the first senator to give birth while in office. She even helped change Senate rules so that she could bring her newborn daughter onto the Senate floor during votes.

Tammy has used her position to fight for veterans, working families, and people with disabilities. She has sponsored bills to help make air travel easier for new mothers, protect the rights of veterans, and improve public transportation.

One of Tammy's most powerful moments came when she stood up to those who questioned her patriotism. She famously said, "I left parts of my body in Iraq fighting terrorists. I don't need to prove my patriotism to anyone."

Another time, she said, "When you say, 'A woman can't do this,' I'm the type to say, 'Hold my beer. Watch this.'" This attitude has helped her break barriers and inspire others throughout her life.

A Voice for Asian Americans and All Americans

As one of only two Asian American women in the U.S. Senate, Tammy is a powerful voice for the Asian American community. She has spoken out against discrimination and worked to ensure that all Americans, regardless of their background, have the opportunity to succeed.

Tammy's story is especially inspiring for young Asian Americans who want to know that it's possible to embrace both their Asian heritage and their American identity.

"I am a daughter of the American Revolution. I'm also a daughter of Thailand. But first and foremost, I am an American."

Continuing to Serve and Inspire

Today, Tammy continues to serve in the U.S. Senate, balancing her work with being a mother to two young daughters. Her journey from a girl who grew up in Southeast Asia to a United States Senator is a powerful reminder that anything is possible with hard work, determination, and a commitment to serving others.

What Ideas Influence Tammy Duckworth?

Her story continues to inspire people of all backgrounds, showing that the American dream is alive and well for those willing to pursue it.

These might be some of the ideas that inspire Tammy:

1. Courage is king.

2. Your dreams are worth fighting for.

3. Serve others before self.

4. Never give up, even when you encounter obstacles.

Think About It

Tammy once said, "It's not about your disabilities, it's about your abilities."

This powerful statement reminds us that we all have unique strengths and talents to offer the world.

What do you think are yours?

SPORTS

CHAMPIONS ON AND OFF THE FIELD

SAMMY LEE

MAKING A SPLASH IN OLYMPIC HISTORY
(1920-2016)

D ue to his racial background, Sammy Lee faced challenges but dove right past them—literally—and became the first Asian American man to win an Olympic gold medal for the United States.

A Diving Dream is Born

Samuel Lee was born on August 1, 1920, in Fresno, California. His parents were Korean immigrants who ran a small Chinese restaurant. When Sammy was 12 years old, something happened that would change his life forever.

The 1932 Summer Olympics came to Los Angeles, and the city was buzzing. Olympic banners and souvenirs were everywhere. That summer, Sammy also discovered he had a special talent—he could do diving somersaults better than all his friends! This discovery, combined with the Olympic fever in the air, sparked a dream in Sammy's heart. He set himself an incredible goal: to become an Olympic champion in diving.

But Sammy's path to the Olympics wouldn't be easy. His family moved to Highland Park, a neighborhood in Los Angeles. There, Sammy faced a huge obstacle. The local public swimming pool only allowed people of color—including Asians, Latinos, and African Americans—to use it one day a week. This was called "International Day," and it happened right before the pool was cleaned and refilled. Sammy needed a place to practice diving, but he couldn't use the pool regularly like the white kids.

Digging Deep for Success

Sammy persevered and found a dedicated coach who refused to let this unfair rule stop his talented student. Sammy's coach dug a pit in his own backyard and filled it with sand, which became Sammy's training ground. He practiced his dives over this pit of sand instead of water. It wasn't ideal, but Sammy was determined to follow his dream, no matter what.

Sammy excelled both in sports and school. He attended Franklin High School and then went on to study at Occidental College where his dedication to diving began to pay off. In 1942, he won the United States National Diving Championships in both the 3-meter springboard and the 10-meter platform events. Sammy became the first person of color to win the national championship in diving!

After earning his undergraduate degree at Occidental College, Sammy enrolled at the University of Southern California School of Medicine and worked to balance his diving career with medical studies. It wasn't easy, but he was determined to succeed in both areas. To help pay for his medical school tuition, he joined the Army Reserve and graduated from medical school in 1947.

Olympic Glory

In 1948, Sammy was selected for the U.S. team for the Summer Olympics in London, England. He was meeting the goal he had made at 12 years old! Sammy's performance was outstanding. He won a bronze medal in the 3-meter springboard event and a gold medal in the 10-meter platform diving!

Sammy Lee became the first Asian American man to win an Olympic gold medal for the United States. He followed Filipino American Vicki Draves, who had won women's springboard diving just two days earlier.

A Historic Double

Four years later, Sammy was ready to defend his Olympic title. By this time, he was a major in the United States Army Medical Corps as a doctor specializing in ear diseases. He was expected to serve in the Korean War but instead was sent to compete in the 1952 Olympic Games in Helsinki, Finland. His commanding officers had one message for him: "You better win!" And win, he did!

Once again, Sammy captured the gold medal in the 10-meter platform competition. With this victory, he became the first man to win back-to-back gold medals in Olympic platform diving.

Diving Through Barriers

Even after the Olympics, in the 1940s and 1950s, Sammy Lee often experienced prejudice as an Asian American. In 1954, he tried to buy a house in Garden Grove, California, but some neighbors petitioned to stop him because of his race. Imagine the hurt he, a U.S. Olympic champion and military veteran, felt!

A Lasting Legacy

After his diving career, Sammy continued to serve others in many ways. As a doctor, he specialized in treating ear, nose, and throat problems, helping countless patients over his 35-year career. He also became a coach, sharing his expertise with the next generation of divers. Among his students were Bob Webster, who won two Olympic gold medals, and Greg Louganis, who went on to become one of the greatest divers in history.

Sammy Lee's achievements have been recognized in many ways. He was inducted into the International Swimming Hall of Fame and the U.S. Olympic Hall of Fame. In Los Angeles, there's even a square named after him in Koreatown! But perhaps his most important legacy is the inspiration he provides to young Asian Americans and all young people who face challenges.

"I tell my kids," he once said, "If you have a job, do it right and do it better than anyone else, and you'll never have to worry about a job."

This advice shows how Sammy approached everything in his life with dedication and a commitment to excellence.

What Ideas Influenced Sammy Lee?

Perhaps Sammy's greatest legacy is the inspiration he provides to others. Here's what he once said about facing challenges:

"I had to overcome prejudice, and I had to overcome my size. I was only 5-feet-2. And I had to overcome the fact that I was an Asian American. But I'm not bitter. I was told that if you worked hard and if you have faith in yourself and use your brains, you could overcome."

His ideas are worth repeating:

1. Work hard.

2. Have faith in yourself.

3. Use your brains.

Think About It

The next time you face a challenge that seems too big to overcome, remember Sammy Lee—the boy who practiced diving in a sandpit and went on to become an Olympic champion and a respected doctor.

What goals do you think you, with determination and courage, could achieve to make your own splash in history?

WATARU MISAKA

BREAKING BARRIERS ON THE BASKETBALL COURT (1923-2019)

W ataru Misaka embodied exceptional courage and talent when he became the first person of color and the first Asian American to play professional basketball in what would become the NBA.

Early Life and Challenges

Wataru Misaka was born on December 21, 1923, in Ogden, Utah. His parents were Japanese immigrants, making Wataru a second-generation Japanese American, or *Nisei*. Wataru's family was poor, living in the basement of his father's barbershop in a rough part of town.

Wataru lived in a time when people treated him differently just because of how he looked. He couldn't join after-school clubs and couldn't eat in some restaurants because of his ethnicity; sometimes, neighbors would even cross the street to avoid him. This kind of unjust treatment was common for many Asian Americans back then.

Despite these obstacles, Wataru found joy and success in sports. He played in Japanese American baseball and basketball leagues, honing his skills and building his confidence. In high school, Wataru's basketball skills really started to shine. As a 5' 7"-tall guard, he led his Ogden High School team to a state championship in 1940 and a regional championship in 1941. Wataru's remarkable journey had just begun.

College Years and Wartime

After high school, Wataru attended Weber College (now Weber State University). His basketball skills continued to impress, and he led the team to two championships. In 1942, he was named the Most Valuable Player of the entire junior college postseason tournament!

Wataru's college years coincided with a dark time in American history—World War II. While many Japanese Americans were forced into internment camps*, Wataru was able to continue his education. He transferred to the University of Utah, joining its basketball team, the Utes. In his first season there, something incredible happened. The team was invited to play in the National Invitation Tournament (NIT) in New York City—a huge deal at the time!

Although they lost their first game, they played in another tournament called the NCAA Tournament. Wataru and his team seized this opportunity and won the whole thing, becoming national NCAA champions!

Wataru's college career was interrupted when he was drafted into the U.S. Army during World War II. He served for two years, rising to the rank of staff sergeant. After the war, he returned to the University of Utah and rejoined the basketball team. In 1947, Wataru and the Utes won that year's National Invitation Tournament in New York. During the final game, Wataru played amazing defense, holding one of the opponent's best players to just a single point!

During World War II, the United States and Japan were enemies. Sadly, this led the U.S. government to make a terrible decision. They forced over 110,000 people of Japanese origin, the majority of them U.S. citizens, to leave their homes and live in guarded camps called internment camps. Most of these people had done nothing wrong and were loyal to America. The government's action was based on fear and prejudice, not facts. Years later, the U.S. admitted this was a big mistake and formally apologized.

Breaking into the Pros

Wataru's talent on the basketball court didn't go unnoticed. In 1947, he was drafted by the New York Knicks, a professional basketball team. Wataru became the first person of color and the first Asian American to play in the Basketball Association of America (which later became the NBA).

In the same year that Jackie Robinson broke the color barrier in baseball, Wataru Misaka was doing the same thing in professional basketball. But unlike Robinson, there wasn't much fanfare around Wataru's debut.

He once said, "It wasn't a big thing. Nobody cared." It would be another three years before the first African American player joined the NBA.

Despite this groundbreaking achievement, Wataru's time with the Knicks was short. He played in just three games, scoring seven points, before being cut from the team. Wataru believed this was simply because the team had too many guards (his position) rather than due to discrimination. In fact, Wataru said he didn't feel any unfair treatment from his teammates or opponents during his time with the Knicks. Still, his brief time in the league paved the way for future generations of diverse players.

Life After Basketball

After his professional basketball career ended, Wataru made a practical decision. He turned down an offer to play with the famous basketball entertainment group, Harlem Globetrotters, and instead returned to the University of Utah to complete his engineering degree.

Wataru explained his choice: "The salary for a rookie and the salary for a starting engineer weren't much different."

After graduating, Wataru worked as an electrical engineer in Salt Lake City for many years. He married his wife, Kate, and had two children. Even though he was no longer playing professional basketball, Wataru continued to enjoy sports. He took up bowling and even bowled a near-perfect game of 299 when he was 80 years old!

Legacy and Impact

Wataru Misaka's achievements didn't receive much attention during his playing days. But as time passed, people began to recognize the importance of what he had done.

In 1999, Wataru was inducted into the Utah Sports Hall of Fame. In 2008, a documentary film about his life, *Transcending: The Wat Misaka Story*, was released. This film helped share Wataru's story with a wider audience, inspiring new generations of Asian Americans and other minorities in sports.

What Ideas Influenced Wataru Misaka?

Wataru's life shows us that sometimes, you can make history quietly. Maybe he set out to break barriers, but maybe he didn't.

Perhaps these ideas influenced Wataru:

1. Pursue your passions.

2. Enjoy the process.

3. Think positive.

4. Every step forward, no matter how small it might seem, matters.

Think About It

Wataru Misaka passed away in 2019 at the age of 95, but his legacy lives on. He was one of the pioneers who helped make diversity on basketball courts possible.

Do you know anybody today who you think is making history quietly?

MICHAEL CHANG

THE YOUNGEST GRAND SLAM CHAMPION
(1972-)

At just 17 years old, Michael Chang achieved what most people only dream of—becoming the best in the world at something. That's exactly what Michael Chang did when he became the youngest male player ever to win a Grand Slam tennis tournament.

A Tennis Prodigy Is Born

Michael Te-Pei Chang was born on February 22, 1972, in Hoboken, New Jersey. His parents, Joe and Betty Chang, had immigrated to the United States from Taiwan. Like many immigrant families, the Changs worked hard to give their children opportunities for success.

When Michael was young, his family moved to Minnesota and then to California, always looking for better chances for Michael and his older brother Carl to play tennis. Michael's talent was clear from an early age. By the time he was 12, he was already setting "youngest-ever" records in junior tennis tournaments.

Even though he was a tennis phenomenon, people sometimes treated Michael differently because of how he looked. But he didn't let that stop him from pursuing his dreams. Instead, he focused on what he loved most: tennis.

Rising to the Top

Michael's dedication to tennis was incredible. He practiced for hours every day, often with his father as his coach. His hard work paid off, and at just 15 years old, he became the youngest player ever to win a match at the U.S. Open, one of the biggest tennis tournaments in the world!

The Miracle Match

Michael's biggest moment came in 1989 when he was 17 years old. He entered the French Open, one of the four most important tennis tournaments in the world. Nobody expected the young player to go very far, but Michael had other expectations.

In one of the most famous matches in tennis history, Michael faced Ivan Lendl, the world's top-ranked player at the time. Michael was losing badly and started to suffer from painful leg cramps. It looked like he might have to give up.

But he didn't quit. Instead, he hit high, looping shots to slow down the game and give himself time to recover. He even surprised fans and his opponent by serving underhanded at a crucial moment! Against all odds, Michael won the match after more than four hours of play. He then went on to win the entire tournament, becoming the youngest male player ever to win a Grand Slam title. He was only 17 years and 110 days old!

Addressing his perseverance, Michael said, "I felt an unbelievable conviction in my heart not to give up."

Challenges and Triumphs

Michael's victory was more than just a personal triumph. He became the first American man to win the French Open in 34 years. Even more importantly, he was the first Asian American man to win a Grand Slam title in tennis.

But winning the French Open at such a young age wasn't always a positive thing for Michael. Suddenly, he was famous, and people expected him to keep winning. The pressure was intense, but Michael stayed focused on his skills and on his game.

Throughout his career, Michael faced challenges because of his size. At 5 feet 9 inches tall, he was shorter than most of his opponents. But instead of seeing this as a disadvantage, Michael used his speed and agility to develop a unique playing style. He became known for his incredible defense and ability to run down almost any shot.

Michael reached the finals of three more Grand Slam tournaments and was ranked as high as number two in the world in 1996.

Impact on the Asian American Community

Michael's victories meant a lot to Asian Americans, and at a time when there weren't many Asian American sports stars, he was a role model for young Asian Americans who dreamed of excelling in sports or any other field.

Interestingly, Michael's 1989 French Open victory came just one day after the Tiananmen Square protests in China*. He later reflected on this timing:

"I think it was God's purpose for me to be able to win the French Open the way it was won because I was able to put a smile on Chinese people's faces around the world at a time when there wasn't much to smile about."

Sports can sometimes have an impact beyond just winning or losing a game.

On June 4, 1979, the Chinese government sent soldiers and tanks to stop peaceful student and worker democracy demonstrations in Tiananmen Square, Beijing. The aggression resulted in violence and loss of life. This event, known as the Tiananmen Square Massacre, was a significant moment in Chinese history and is still a sensitive topic in China today.

Beyond the Tennis Court

Michael's impact went beyond the tennis court. He used his fame to inspire young people and to help others. He supported programs to help develop young tennis players in Asia and worked with charities in the United States.

After he retired from professional tennis in 2003, Michael became a coach, helping other players improve their skills. He even wrote a book about his life and career called *Holding Serve: Persevering On and Off the Court*.

Inspiring the Next Generation

Michael once said, "Simply by being out there, I think I made a difference in people's perceptions about Asian athletes."

In a world where Asian Americans are still underrepresented in many sports, Michael's success shows that barriers can be broken—for Asian Americans and for all underrepresented populations.

What Ideas Influence Michael Chang?

Michael's journey certainly reminds us that no matter your ancestry or what you look like, you can achieve your dreams with hard work and perseverance. But specific ideas seem to inspire him, such as:

1. Set your goals.

2. Show up, every day, for your passions.

3. Identify your weaknesses and make them strengths.

4. Give it everything you've got.

Think About It

So, are you ready to pick up your racket (or paintbrush, or calculator, or whatever tool you need for your dreams) to start making history?

MICHELLE KWAN

COMPETITIVE FIGURE SKATER TURNED DIPLOMAT (1980-)

P icture this: A young girl glides across the ice, her heart pounding with a dream so big it could barely fit in the enormous skating rinks where she practiced. That girl was Michelle Kwan, and she didn't just dream of being good—she aimed at being the best figure skater the world had ever seen.

A Star is Born

Michelle Wingshan Kwan was born on July 7, 1980, in Torrance, California. Her parents, Danny and Estella Kwan, were immigrants from Hong Kong. Growing up, Michelle spoke both English and Cantonese at home, connecting her to her Chinese heritage.

Michelle first stepped onto the ice at just five years old, following in the footsteps of her older siblings. Little did anyone know that this would be the beginning of an incredible journey. When she was eight, she and her sister Karen began serious training, waking up at 4:30 a.m. to practice before school and returning to the rink after school.

Michelle's path to success wasn't without its bumps and bruises (literally)! Paying for expensive coaching and ice time was a financial struggle for the Kwan family. There were times when they couldn't pay for a coach at all. But Michelle's talent and determination shone through. When she was ten, a fellow skater's family offered to help with expenses, allowing Michelle to train at a top facility in Lake Arrowhead, California.

Rising to the Top

Michelle's hard work began to pay off. At just 13 years old, she qualified for the 1994 U.S. Figure Skating Championships, finishing second. Although she didn't compete at the Olympics that year, it was clear that a new star was on the rise. In 1996, at age 15, Michelle won her first World Championship title. This was just the beginning of an incredible career.

Over the next decade, Michelle dominated the world of figure skating. She won an incredible nine U.S. Championships and five World Championships. At the 1998 Olympics in Nagano, Japan, Michelle won a silver medal, and four years later in Salt Lake City, she added a bronze to her collection.

But Michelle's impact went beyond her medals. She was known for her grace, artistry, and consistency on the ice. Fans and fellow skaters admired her for her "silent blades"—the quiet, smooth way she glided across the ice. Her signature move, a beautiful spiral where she changed edges while gliding on one foot, became legendary in the skating world. She wasn't just a great athlete; she was a true performer!

Overcoming Challenges

The pressure of being a top athlete was intense for Michelle, and she had to balance training with school and a normal teenage life. As an Asian American, she sometimes also felt the weight of representing her community on the world stage.

And like any great story, Michelle's journey had its share of disappointments. Despite being a favorite to win gold at the 1998 and 2002 Olympics, she came away with silver and bronze medals instead. Many athletes might have been crushed, but not Michelle. She showed true sportsmanship and resilience, continuing to compete and inspire others.

In 2006, Michelle faced perhaps her biggest challenge. After earning a spot on the Olympic team, she suffered an injury during practice in Turin, Italy. Instead of competing as she desperately wanted to, she made the difficult decision to withdraw—because she knew she would not be able to compete at the level where she should. Michelle said, "I respect the Olympics too much to compete."

Michelle could show integrity and respect for her sport, even in a heartbreaking moment.

Impact and Inspiration

Michelle's influence extended far beyond the ice rink. As one of the most famous Asian American athletes of her time, she became a role model for many young people, especially those of Asian descent.

"When I was competing, I didn't realize how much of an impact I was having on the Asian American community," Michelle once said. "Now, I hear from so many people who say they started skating because of me or felt proud to see someone who looked like them succeeding on the world stage."

Michelle's success helped break stereotypes and showed that Asian Americans could excel in any field. She appeared on magazine covers, starred in TV specials, and even had her own video game! Through it all, she remained humble and committed to her sport and her heritage.

A New Chapter

After retiring from competitive skating, Michelle didn't slow down. She graduated from the University of Denver with a degree in international studies and later earned a master's degree from Tufts University. She became involved in diplomacy, serving as a public diplomacy ambassador for the U.S. State Department. In this role, Michelle traveled the world, using her fame and experience to connect with young people and promote understanding between cultures. She visited countries like China, Russia, and South Korea, showing how sports can bring people together across borders.

In 2022, Michelle took on a new challenge when President Joe Biden appointed her as the U.S. Ambassador to Belize. This made her the first Asian American woman to hold this position, once again breaking barriers and representing her community.

What Ideas Influence Michelle Kwan?

There are two influential ideas that Michelle Kwan's life embodies that stand out:

1. Setbacks don't define you—it's how you respond to them that matters.

2. Your skills in one area (like sports) can open doors in unexpected places (like diplomacy).

Think About It

Michelle has said, "I always thought, 'What if I don't make it?' I had to have a backup plan."

Michelle balanced her big dreams with practical thinking. It's a great reminder that it's okay to have big goals, but it's also smart to prepare for different possibilities.

What are your big goals right now? What if you don't achieve them? How could making the goals positively affect other possibilities?

APOLO OHNO

SKATING TO OLYMPIC GLORY (1982-)

B lazing across the ice at lightning speeds, short-track speed skaters captivated audiences worldwide during the Winter Olympics but one name stands out: Apolo Ohno. This Asian American athlete became one of the most decorated Winter Olympians in U.S. history.

A Unique Beginning

Born on May 22, 1982, in Seattle, Washington, Apolo has a name that tells a story. His father chose "Apolo" based on the Greek words "apo," meaning "steer away from," and "lo," meaning "look out, here he comes!"

Apolo's father, Yuki Ohno, immigrated to the United States from Japan, and his mother was European-American, but not a big part of his life. Growing up without his mother wasn't easy, but Apolo and his dad formed a close bond.

As a young boy, Apolo was full of energy. Yuki worked long hours as a hairstylist to support his son, often leaving Apolo alone after school. Worried that Apolo would become an unproductive "latchkey kid" (a child who spends a lot of time alone at home), Yuki decided to get his son involved in different sports.

Fun Fact: Apolo can speak three languages: English, French, and Korean!

Finding His Passion

At first, Apolo tried swimming and inline speed skating. He was good at both, becoming a state champion in breaststroke swimming and even a national inline skating champion. But everything changed when 12-year-old Apolo watched the 1994 Winter Olympics short-track speed skating on TV. He was instantly hooked.

Apolo begged his dad to let him try speed skating. Yuki, always supportive, began driving Apolo to competitions all over the northwest United States and Canada. Soon, Apolo was winning races in his age group.

The Road to Olympic Glory

When he was just 14 years old, Apolo became the youngest skater ever admitted to the Olympic Training Center in Lake Placid, New York, and moved there to train full-time. At first, Apolo struggled with the intense training. His teammates even nicknamed him "Chunky" because he wasn't in the best shape.

Instead of giving up, Apolo used the experience as motivation to work harder. He transformed his body and his skills, becoming the youngest person ever to win the U.S. Senior Championships in 1997 at age 14!

Despite this early success, Apolo faced a major setback when he failed to qualify for the 1998 Winter Olympics. Many people might have given up after such a disappointment, but not Apolo. He doubled down on his training, determined to make the next Olympic team.

Olympic Triumphs and Challenges

Apolo's hard work paid off at the 2002 Winter Olympics in Salt Lake City. He won his first gold medal in the 1500-meter race, but it came with controversy. The first-place finisher, representing South Korea, was disqualified, moving Apolo from silver to gold. Some people, especially in South Korea, were angry about this decision. Apolo received many negative messages and even death threats. Apolo chose to focus on his skating and not let the criticism bring him down.

In the same Olympics, Apolo also won a silver medal in a dramatic 1000-meter race where several skaters crashed near the finish line. This race showed how exciting and unpredictable short-track speed skating can be.

Apolo wasn't finished. He went on to compete in two more Winter Olympics. In 2006, in Turin, Italy, he won gold in the 500-meter race and two bronze medals. Then, in 2010, in Vancouver, Canada, he added two more medals to his collection, bringing his total to eight Olympic medals. This made him the most decorated American Winter Olympian in history at the time.

What's truly remarkable about Apolo's Olympic journey is how he contin-ued to improve and challenge himself. For the 2010 Vancouver Olympics, he underwent an intense five-month training program, losing 20 pounds and getting into the best shape of his life at age 27.

He said, "Come these Games, there's no one who's going to be fitter than me. There's just no way."

Beyond the Ice

Apolo's impact goes far beyond his medal count. He became the face of short-track speed skating in the United States, helping to popularize the sport. He became a role model for aspiring athletes, especially Asian

Americans who didn't see many people who looked like them in winter sports.

He once said, "It's amazing being able to be a role model to younger skaters. Growing up, I did not have that influence within my sport."

In 2007, he won the reality TV show, *Dancing with the Stars*, showing that his grace on the ice translated well to the dance floor. After retiring from competitive skating, Apolo didn't slow down. He's also worked as a sports commentator, appeared in TV shows, and even hosted a game show.

Apolo has used his fame to support important causes. He's raised money for organizations that help elderly Japanese Americans, promoted education in math and science, and worked with the Special Olympics. He also created the Apolo Anton Ohno Foundation to encourage kids to live healthy lifestyles and stay away from underage drinking.

Inspiring a New Generation

Today, Apolo Ohno is remembered not just as a great athlete, but as someone who changed his sport and inspired a generation. He continues to inspire others as an entrepreneur and motivational speaker. He encourages young people to find their passion and work hard to achieve their goals, just like he did.

What Ideas Influence Apolo Ohno?

"It's not about the medal. It's not about the performance," Apolo once said. "It's about pushing yourself to the limit and seeing how far you can go. It's about me looking back and saying I gave it everything I had. I gave it my all."

Apolo Ohno is a motivational speaker whose ideas are very clear.

1. Push yourself.

2. See how far you can go.

3. Give it your all.

Think About It

So, how far can you go? Can you work hard enough towards your goals so you can look back and say, "I gave it my all?"

JEREMY LIN

DEFYING EXPECTATIONS ON AND OFF THE COURT (1988-)

J eremy Lin, the Taiwanese American hoops wizard, faced doubters at every turn. So, Jeremy dribbled, shot, and hustled his way into the NBA, shocking the world and inspiring millions of kids to believe in themselves.

Early Life and Background

Jeremy Shu-How Lin was born on August 23, 1988, in Torrance, California. His parents, Gie-ming and Shirley Lin, had immigrated to the United States from Taiwan in the 1970s. Jeremy grew up in the San Francisco Bay Area city of Palo Alto with his two brothers, Josh and Joseph.

From a young age, Jeremy loved basketball. His father taught him and his brothers to play at the local YMCA. Jeremy's mother also supported his passion, helping to form a youth basketball program where he could play. However, some people discouraged her, saying, "He's Asian, he's supposed to be good at math, not basketball." But she saw how much joy it brought Jeremy and continued to support his dream.

As an Asian American kid playing basketball, Jeremy often stood out. He faced racist taunts from opponents and spectators, who would shout things like "Go back to China!" or "Open your eyes!" But instead of letting these comments bring him down, Jeremy used them as motivation to work even harder to prove people wrong.

In high school, Jeremy led his team to a state championship and was named Northern California Player of the Year. But despite his success, no major college offered him a basketball scholarship. Many people thought he wasn't athletic enough to play at a high level, which Jeremy believed was partly due to stereotypes about Asian athletes.

The Road from Harvard to the NBA

Undeterred, Jeremy enrolled at Harvard University, where he could play basketball while getting an excellent education. He worked tirelessly to improve his skills and eventually became one of the best players in the Ivy League, earning all-conference honors three times.

Jeremy graduated in 2010 with a degree in economics. However, despite his impressive college basketball career, no NBA team drafted him, and his dream of playing professional basketball was slipping away.

But Jeremy refused to give up. He signed with his hometown team, the Golden State Warriors, as an undrafted free agent in 2010. That made him the first American of Chinese or Taiwanese descent to play in the NBA. But he spent most of his time on the bench.

For two years, he bounced between NBA teams and the Development League, never quite finding his place. Both the Warriors and the Houston

Rockets chose to let him go before the New York Knicks hired him in December 2011.

"I'm not playing to prove anything to anybody," Jeremy once said. "I'm playing because I love the game of basketball."

Driven to Linsanity

At first, it looked like Jeremy's NBA dream might be over. He was close to being cut by the Knicks and was sleeping on his brother's couch in a tiny New York apartment. But in February 2012, everything changed.

One night, Jeremy was given an unexpected chance to play due to injuries on the team. Then, magic happened! Jeremy exploded onto the scene, leading the Knicks to a seven-game winning streak, scoring more points in his first five career starts than any player since 1976. He scored 25 points in his first game as a starter, then 28 in the next game, and an incredible 38 points against Kobe Bryant and the Los Angeles Lakers!

Fans and the media went wild, calling this phenomenon "Linsanity." Suddenly, Jeremy Lin appeared on magazine covers and late-night talk shows. He became a global sensation. He appeared on the cover of Sports Illustrated two weeks in a row and was named one of Time magazine's 100 most influential people that year. People all over the world, especially in Asian communities, were so excited and inspired by his story of perseverance and success.

Overcoming Adversity

After his breakout season with the Knicks, Jeremy played for several more NBA teams. Even so, he faced setbacks, battled injuries, and sometimes struggled to find a consistent role. But he never gave up, always working to improve his game and contribute to his team.

In 2019, he became the first Asian American player to win an NBA championship as part of the Toronto Raptors team.

Continuing to Inspire

Jeremy's 2012 magical and historic two-week run with the Knicks became a source of hope and inspiration for everyone, far beyond the basketball court.

When the COVID-19 pandemic closed New York City in early 2020, the city was in desperate need of something positive. MSG Network turned to Linsanity. For an entire week from late April to early May 2020, they replayed the Linsanity games, bringing a much-needed dose of excitement and joy to a city in crisis. Years after it first captivated the world, Linsanity once again became a feel-good story that cheered up countless New Yorkers and basketball fans.

During the pandemic, Jeremy spoke out against racism targeting Asian Americans and donated money to help those affected by the tragedy.

"At a time like this that requires everyone uniting to survive, COVID-19 shouldn't be about East vs. West, politics, race, or anything other than helping as many people as we can survive," Jeremy wrote.

Jeremy Lin has become a symbol of hope and inspiration for Asian Americans and people of all backgrounds who face discrimination or doubt.

What Ideas Influence Jeremy Lin?

Today, Jeremy Lin continues to play professional basketball, most recently in Taiwan's P. League+. Despite his fame, Jeremy remains grounded in his faith, values, and core ideas like these:

1. Follow your passions.

2. Defy expectations.

3. Make a positive impact on the world.

Think About It

"I'm proud of being Asian-American, and I love it," Jeremy said. "I think it's something that gives me a chip on my shoulder."

What do you think Jeremy meant when he said that?

CHLOE KIM

SNOWBOARDING SUPERSTAR AND OLYMPIC CHAMPION (2000-)

S oaring through the air, defying gravity, breaking records, and making history—that's just another day for Chloe Kim on her snowboard.

A California Girl with Olympic Dreams

Chloe Kim was born on April 23, 2000, in Long Beach, California. She grew up in nearby Torrance with her parents and two older sisters. Like many Asian American kids, Chloe came from a family of immigrants. Her parents had moved to the United States from South Korea, hoping to build a better life for their children.

Chloe's journey to snowboarding stardom began when she was just four years old. Her dad, Jong Jin Kim, decided to take her snowboarding at a local resort called Mountain High. Little did he know that this fun family outing would be the start of something incredible!

At first, snowboarding was just a fun way for Chloe to spend time with her dad. But from the moment she strapped on a snowboard, it was clear she had a special talent. By six years old, she was already competing in snowboarding events.

In third grade, Chloe moved to Geneva, Switzerland, to live with her aunt and train in the Swiss Alps. Imagine having to leave your friends and school behind to follow your passion at such a young age! After two years there (where she became fluent in French, on top of her English and Korean), Chloe returned to California and started training at Mammoth Mountain. Her dad made a big sacrifice, too—he quit his job to drive Chloe to the mountains and travel with her to competitions!

Rising to the Top

In 2014, at just 13 years old, Chloe entered the X Games, one of the biggest competitions in action sports. She earned a silver medal in the superpipe event, coming in second only to Kelly Clark, a legendary snow-boarder who had been competing since before Chloe was born.

The very next year, at age 14, she returned to the X Games and won gold, beating Kelly Clark and becoming the youngest gold medalist in X Games history at the time. But Chloe wasn't done breaking records. In 2016, at the age of 15, she became the first person under 16 to win two gold medals at an X Games. She was also the first woman to land back-to-back 1080 spins in a competition. That's three full rotations in the air, twice in a row!

Breaking Barriers and Making History

In 2018, at just 17 years old, Chloe competed in her first Winter Olympics in Pyeongchang, South Korea. This was extra special for Chloe because it was the country her parents had come from.

Chloe didn't just compete—she *dominated*. She won the gold medal in the halfpipe event, making her the youngest woman ever to win an Olympic snowboarding gold medal. Her final run was almost perfect, scoring 98.25 out of 100 points. Chloe had made history!

Being a world-famous athlete at a young age isn't easy. After her first Olympic win, Chloe decided to take a break from competing to go to college. In 2019, she enrolled at Princeton University, one of the best schools in the country. But balancing fame, schoolwork, and snowboarding was tough. Chloe eventually decided to focus on snowboarding again and left school to train.

At the 2022 Winter Olympics in Beijing, China, Chloe came back with a roar. She won another gold medal in the halfpipe, becoming the first woman to win back-to-back Olympic golds in this event.

Chloe cemented her place as one of the greatest snowboarders of all time.

Facing Challenges On and Off the Snow

Despite her incredible success, Chloe's experience hasn't always been positive. Like many Asian Americans, she has faced racism and discrimination. Even though she was born in the United States and has always represented the country in competitions, Chloe has received hurtful messages telling her to "go back to China" or accusing her of "taking medals away from white American girls."

Chloe has spoken openly about these experiences, saying, "I experience hate on a daily basis alongside celebratory messages. It's terrifying."

She has also expressed concern about the rise in anti-Asian hate crimes in recent years, worrying about the safety of her parents and other Asian Americans.

But Chloe remains positive and determined. She uses her platform to speak out against racism and inspire other young Asian Americans to pursue their dreams. Chloe once said, "I'm starting to understand that I can represent both countries." She's proud of her Korean heritage and her American upbringing, showing that you can embrace all parts of your identity.

Inspiring a New Generation

In 2018, Chloe was named one of Time magazine's 100 Most Influential People. She has appeared on the cover of Sports Illustrated and even had her own Barbie doll made in her likeness!

But for Chloe, it's not about the fame or the awards. It's about pushing herself to be the best she can be and inspiring others along the way. She once said, "I want to be a good influence on those younger than me. I want them to feel like they can accomplish anything they set their minds to."

What Ideas Inspire Chloe Kim?

Every time Chloe falls on the snow, she gets back up and tries again. A main idea that inspires her comes directly from one of her quotes:

"Don't be afraid to fall. It's how we learn and how we get better."

Think About It

Chloe continues to push the boundaries in snowboarding, always working on new tricks and ways to improve. Beyond sports, she has worked with major fashion brands and is passionate about using her voice to make a positive difference in the world.

Whether you're learning a new skill, standing up for what you believe in, or working towards a big goal ... What dreams do you have that might seem impossible right now?

... AND MORE

SO WHAT?

NOW WHAT?

As we wrap up our journey through the lives of remarkable Asian Americans, let's reflect on the incredible stories we've explored. From scientists and artists to athletes and activists, each person has left a unique mark on American history and culture. Their stories show how diversity makes our country stronger and more vibrant. It brings *everybody* up.

Key Themes: The Building Blocks of Inspiration

Throughout this book, we've seen several important themes emerge:

1. Perseverance. Many of our heroes faced big challenges like discrimination or poverty. But they didn't give up! They kept working hard toward their goals, even when things got tough.

2. Innovation. These trailblazers weren't afraid to think differently. They often came up with new ideas or found creative solutions to problems.

3. Cultural Pride. While embracing their American identity, many also celebrated their Asian heritage. They showed that you can be proud of all parts of who you are!

4. Breaking Barriers. Almost all these Asian Americans were "firsts" in some way. They opened doors in fields where people who looked like them hadn't been before.

5. Giving Back. Success wasn't just about personal achievements. Many used their talents and influence to help others and make their communities better.

6. Lifelong Learning. Our heroes showed that education doesn't stop when you leave school. They kept growing and learning throughout their lives.

Looking to the Future

The stories in this book are just a small sample of how Asian Americans have shaped, and continue to shape, our country. As you think about your own dreams and goals, remember that we are all part of this American story. You have the power to make your own mark on the world, just like the inspiring people you've read about.

Maybe you'll be inspired by the scientific curiosity of Steven Chu or the artistic vision of Maya Lin. You might feel a connection to the athletic determination of Michelle Kwan or the entrepreneurial spirit of Jerry Yang.

Whatever path you choose, know that these trailblazers have helped pave the way. They've shown that Asian Americans can excel in any field and, like them, your unique background and experiences are valuable assets.

Think About It

1. Which Asian American featured in this book inspired you the most? Why?

2. Why do you think it's important to have diversity in areas like

science, politics, arts, and sports?

3. How did the people we read about overcome obstacles? What can we learn from their experiences?

Keep Exploring!

Want to learn even more about Asian American achievements and culture? Here are some ideas:

- **Visit a museum:** Many cities have museums or cultural centers focused on Asian American history and art.

- **Read more biographies:** Your local library probably has lots of books about other inspiring Asian Americans.

- **Watch documentaries:** There are many great films that explore Asian American experiences and achievements.

- **Attend cultural festivals:** These can be fun ways to experience music, dance, food, and traditions.

- **Learn a language:** Consider studying an Asian language. Even learning a few words can help you connect with different cultures.

Your Story Matters

As we close this book, remember that history is still being written, and you can be part of it! The Asian Americans we've learned about didn't start out famous or powerful. They were once kids just like you, with dreams, fears, and endless potential.

What will your contribution to the world be? Maybe you'll make a scientific discovery, create moving art, or become a leader who fights for justice. Maybe you'll be a compassionate friend or neighbor who will help someone else achieve greatness. Whatever path you choose, know that your unique experiences and perspectives matter.

Embrace your heritage and background, chase your passions, and don't be afraid to be a trailblazer. Persevere through challenges, think creatively, be proud of who you are, and use your talents to make a positive difference.

Your journey is just beginning, and the possibilities are endless!

OTHER NOTABLE ASIAN AMERICANS

AND THE LIST KEEPS GROWING...

A s you've seen throughout this book, Asian Americans have made incredible contributions to our world in so many different fields. While I wish I could have dedicated a full chapter to every inspiring Asian American, there just wasn't enough space!

In this section, I want to introduce you to even more amazing Asian Americans who have changed our world for the better. I've tried my best to include people from many different Asian backgrounds and all genders. You'll find scientists, artists, athletes, politicians, and more!

In parentheses, I noted their ethnic ancestry or lineage on the Asian side. But remember, they are/were all proud Americans, just like you and me!

Film & Television

- **Philip Ahn** (Korean, 1905-1978): Actor and activist

- **Miyoshi Umeki** (Japanese, 1929-2007): Singer and actor; first East Asia-born woman to win an Academy Award for acting

- **James Hong** (Chinese, 1929-): Actor, producer, and director

- **Pat Morita** (Japanese, 1932-2005): Actor/comedian known for *Happy Days* and *The Karate Kid*

- **George Takei** (Japanese, 1937-): Actor of *Star Trek* fame, LGBT activist

- **Haing S. Ngor** (Cambodian, 1940–1996): Actor and medical doctor; won the Academy Award for Best Supporting Actor in 1985.

- **Wayne Wang** (Chinese, 1949-): Film director, producer, and screenwriter

- **Margaret Cho** (Korean, 1968-): Actress/comedian

- **Carrie Ann Inaba** (Japanese, 1968-): Television personality, dancer, choreographer, actress, and singer

- **M. Night Shyamalan** (Indian, 1970-): Film director, producer, and screenwriter

- **Padma Lakshmi** (Indian, 1970-): Author, model, activist, and television host

- **Sandra Oh** (Korean, 1971-): Actress in *Grey's Anatomy* and numerous films

- **Jon M. Chu** (Chinese/Taiwanese, 1979-): Film director, producer, and screenwriter

Music, Art, and Design

- **Yasuo Kuniyoshi** (Japanese, 1889-1953): Painter, photographer and printmaker

- **Isamu Noguchi** (Japanese, 1904-1988): Artist, sculptor, landscape architect, and furniture designer

- **Toshiko Akiyoshi** (Japanese, 1929-): Jazz pianist, composer/arranger, and bandleader

- **Nam June Paik** (Korean, 1932-2006): Artist, sculptor; "Father of Video Art"

- **Anna Sui** (Chinese, 1955-): Fashion designer

- **Bruno Mars** (Filipino, 1985-): Singer-songwriter, performer, and music producer

Literature and Journalism

- **Maxine Hong Kingston** (Chinese, 1940-): Novelist best known for *The Woman Warrior*

- **Connie Chung** (Chinese, 1946-): News program anchor and journalist

- **Amy Tan** (Chinese, 1952-): Author best known for her novel *The Joy Luck Club*

- **Linda Sue Park** (Korean, 1960-): Newbery Medal-winning author of children's novels and picture books

- **Fareed Zakaria** (Indian, 1964-): Journalist, political commentator, and author.

- **Gene Luen Yang** (Chinese, 1973-): Cartoonist/graphic novelist; MacArthur Fellowship recipient

Science & Technology

- **Margaret Chung** (Chinese, 1889-1959): The first American-born Chinese female doctor

- **Subrahmanyan Chandrasekhar** (Indian, 1910-1995): Nobel Prize-winning theoretical physicist

- **Narinder S. Kapany** (Indian, 1926-2020): Physicist, known as the "Father of Fiber Optics"

- **Amar Boze** (Indian, 1929-2013): Entrepreneur, academic, electrical engineer, and sound engineer; founder of Boze Corporation

- **Samuel Chao Chung Ting** (Chinese, 1936-): Nobel Prize-winning physicist

- **Daniel C. Tsui** (Chinese, 1939-): Nobel Prize-winning physicist

- **Wen Ho Lee** (Taiwanese, 1939-): Nuclear scientist and mechanical engineer

- **Ellison Onizuka** (Japanese, 1946-1986): Astronaut and engineer; first Asian American and the first person of Japanese origin to reach space

- **Michio Kaku** (Japanese, 1947-): Theoretical physicist, science communicator, and futurologist

Business

- **Indra Nooyi** (Indian, 1955-): Businesswoman; CEO of Pepsico 2006-2018

- **Weili Dai** (Chinese, 1962-): Businesswoman; co-founder, former director and former president of Marvell Technology Group

- **Jen-Hsun Huang** (Taiwanese, 1963-): Businessman and electrical engineer, serving as the president and CEO of Nvidia

Activism & Politics

- **S. I. Hayakawa** (Japanese, 1906-1992): Professor of English, President of San Francisco State University, and U.S. Senator

- **Hiram Fong** (Chinese, 1906-2004): The first Asian-American United States Senator, serving 1959-1977

- **Yuri Kochiyama** (Japanese, 1921-2014): Civil rights activist

- **Norman Mineta** (Japanese, 1931-2022): Former Secretary of Commerce and Secretary of Transportation; the first Asian American to serve in a presidential cabinet

- **Eric Shinseki** (Japanese, 1942-): The first Asian-American four-star general, and the first Asian-American Secretary of Veterans Affairs

- **Bobby Scott** (Filipino, 1947-): Lawyer and politician; first Filipino American voting member of Congress

- **Piyush "Bobby" Jindal** (Indian, 1971-): Politician who served as the 55th governor of Louisiana from 2008 to 2016

- **Nikki Haley** (Indian, 1972-): Politician and diplomat

- **Andrew Yang** (Taiwanese, 1975-): Businessman, attorney, lobbyist, author, and politician

Sports

- **Vicki Draves** (Filipino, 1924-2010): Diver; first Asian American—woman or man—to win Olympic gold medals

- **Kristi Yamaguchi** (Japanese, 1971-): Competitive figure skater (Olympic gold medalist), author, and philanthropist

- **Jeanette Lee** (Korean, 1971-): World-ranking professional pool player

- **Tiger Woods** (Thai, 1975-): Golfer

- **Nathan Chen** (Chinese, 1999-): Competitive figure skater and Olympic gold medalist

Remember, this list is still just the tip of the iceberg. There are so many more incredible Asian Americans out there making a difference every day. My sincerest hope is that you'll be inspired to learn more about some of these people, or even to become a trailblazer yourself one day!

REFERENCES

10 minutes with Ken Jeong | Duke Mag. (2024, February 27). Duke Mag.
https://dukemag.duke.edu/stories/10-minutes-ken-jeong

About Apolo Anton Ohno | Olympic speed skater to businessman. (n.d.).
https://www.apoloohno.com/about

Academy of Achievement. (2022, November 22). *Maya Lin | Academy of Achievement.*
https://achievement.org/achiever/maya-lin/

Ahmed, K. (2024, May 16). *The life, career, and accomplishments of cellist Yo-Yo Ma — Stage Music Center in Acton and Winchester MA.* Stage Music Center in Acton and Winchester MA.
https://stagemusiccenter.com/music-school-blog-winchester-acton-ma/yp-yo-ma-biography

Biography: Anna May Wong. (n.d.). Biography: Anna May Wong.
https://www.womenshistory.org/education-resources/biographies/anna-may-wong

Biography: historical and celebrity profiles. (n.d.). Biography. https://www.biography.com/

BIOGRAPHY. (n.d.). http://architecture-history.org/architects/architects/PEI/biography.html

Biography | Yo-Yo Ma. (n.d.). https://www.yo-yoma.com/biography/

Chin, D. (2022, February 4). The Legacy of Linsanity, 10 years later. *The Ringer.*
https://www.theringer.com/nba/2022/2/4/22916972/jeremy-lin-linsanity-knicks-asian-american-representation-10th-anniversary

Dr. Steven Chu. (n.d.). Energy.gov. https://www.energy.gov/person/dr-steven-chu

Early Life and Background · Deconstructing the Model Minority at UM · aapi. (n.d.).
https://aapi.umhistorylabs.lsa.umich.edu/s/aapi_michigan/page/early-life

Empowering students to pursue their passions. (n.d.). Tiger Woods.
https://tigerwoods.com/biography/

Famous African Americans. (n.d.). *Tiger Woods - Biography and facts.* FAMOUS AFRICAN AMERICANS. https://www.famousafricanamericans.org/tiger-woods

Famous athletes. (2024, July 16). Biography. https://www.biography.com/athletes/

Gold House. (2022, May 2). *Chloe Kim | Gold House.* https://goldhouse.org/people/chloe-kim-3/

Grace Lee Boggs. (n.d.). Rise up for Asian Americans and Pacific Islanders - Spotlight at Stanford. https://exhibits.stanford.edu/riseup/feature/grace-lee-boggs

Gyure, D. A. (2020, July 26). *Minoru Yamasaki (1912-1986) - The Architectural Review.* The Architectural Review.
https://www.architectural-review.com/essays/reputations/minoru-yamasaki-1912-1986

History and culture. (2024, July 17). Biography. https://www.biography.com/history-culture

Holt, C. (2023, January 11). Wataru Misaka: the Utah native who broke sports barriers. *KSL Sports.* https://kslsports.com/493896/wataru-misaka-utah-basketball-history/

Huang, C. L. (2018). Roger Yonchien Tsien. 1 February 1952—24 August 2016. *Biographical Memoirs of Fellows of the Royal Society, 65*, 405–428. https://doi.org/10.1098/rsbm.2018.0013

International Tennis Hall of Fame. (n.d.). https://www.tennisfame.com/hall-of-famers/inductees/michael-chang

Kalpana Chawla: the first South Asian American woman in space. (2023, February 1). National Air and Space Museum. https://airandspace.si.edu/stories/editorial/kalpana-chawla

Louise. (2024, March 11). A principled politician: The story of Patsy Mink, the first woman of color elected to Congress. *University of Chicago News.* https://news.uchicago.edu/story/principled-politician-story-patsy-mink-first-woman-color -elected-congress

Malach, H. (2023, November 3). How Vera Wang Went From Ice Skater to the A-List Crowd's Top Bridal Designer. *WWD.* https://wwd.com/feature/vera-wang-history-1235909839/

Meet Tammy - Tammy Duckworth for U.S. Senate. (2023, November 30). Tammy Duckworth for U.S. Senate. https://tammyduckworth.com/meet-tammy/

Meet the cinematographer who changed films forever - Google Arts & Culture. (n.d.). Google Arts & Culture. https://artsandculture.google.com/story/meet-the-cinematographer-who-changed-films-fo rever/DALS5WZQPEMDKg

Movies and TV. (2024, July 18). Biography. https://www.biography.com/movies-tv

The National Museum of American Diplomacy. (2023, September 28). *Dr. Sammy Lee: Olympic Champion and Goodwill Ambassador - The National Museum of American Diplomacy.* https://diplomacy.state.gov/stories/dr-sammy-lee-olympic-champion-and-goodwill-ambas sador/

National Museum of the United States Army. (n.d.). https://www.thenmusa.org/biographies/daniel-k-inouye/

Olympians: The most noteworthy Olympic athletes throughout history. (2024, July 16). Biography. https://www.biography.com/olympic-athletes

Roth, M. S., & Roth, M. S. (2024, April 30). *Anna May Wong: 13 facts about her trailblazing Hollywood career.* HISTORY. https://www.history.com/news/anna-may-wong-facts-career

Who was Dalip Singh Saund? (n.d.). Wonderopolis. https://wonderopolis.org/wonder/Who-Was-Dalip-Singh-Saund

Wikipedia contributors. (2024, May 23). *Main page.* https://en.wikipedia.org/wiki/

Women in radiation History: Chien-Shiung Wu | US EPA. (2023, November 30). US EPA. https://www.epa.gov/radtown/women-radiation-history-chien-shiung-wu

WSU Yamasaki Legacy- Minoru Yamasaki biography. (n.d.). http://yamasaki.wayne.edu/biography.html

Yang, Jerry | Encyclopedia.com. (n.d.). https://www.encyclopedia.com/education/economics-magazines/yang-jerry

IMAGE ATTRIBUTION

ABOUT THE AUTHOR

Mari Yamaguchi is a first-generation Japanese American author, born in Japan and raised in the New York suburbs. She lived for several years in the San Francisco Bay Area, where Asian Americans form a significant part of the population. When she returned to the East Coast, she witnessed differences in how Asian Americans are perceived across the country.

Now, as a mother raising a biracial child in Brooklyn, NY, Mari is deeply aware of the challenges facing children growing up in a predominantly white society. Because she understands that children of color need to see themselves in role models, Mari wrote *Inspiring Asian Americans: 30 Role Models Who Shaped Our World—Past and Present.* She hopes her young readers will find pride in their heritages, curiosity, excitement, and hope for their futures.

When she's not writing, Mari and her daughter enjoy exploring her daughter's rich Japanese and Italian heritages in New York City's vibrant cultural scene.

Did You Enjoy This Book?

Hey there! If you found inspiration in these stories of amazing Asian Americans, why not **share that feeling with others? Your review can help other kids** discover these amazing people too! It's super easy to leave a review:

1. In the US, UK, or Canada, **scan** the QR code above with your phone or tablet. Otherwise, **find this book in your Digital Orders** on Amazon, scroll down, and click the "Write a customer review" button.

2. Leave **a star rating**. You can stop right there, or you can also...

3. Share what you liked about the book! This can be short and sweet - **even a sentence or two** helps!

Remember, **your voice matters!** By sharing what you thought, you can:

- Help other kids find a book they might love

- Let me know what kinds of stories you want to read more about

- Inspire more books about amazing Asian Americans

Thank you in advance for sharing your thoughts!

Love,

Mari

To purchase another copy of this book,

just scan this QR code!

www.ingramcontent.com/pod-product-compliance
Lightning Source LLC
Chambersburg PA
CBHW060039150626
46553CB00017BA/591